ALL ABOUT RADIATION

L. RON HUBBARD

with Dr. Gene Denk and Dr. Farley R. Spink

ALL ABOUT RADIATION

new·era®
Publications International ApS

A **HUBBARD**® PUBLICATION

Published by
NEW ERA® Publications International ApS
Store Kongensgade 55
1264 Copenhagen K, Denmark

This book is part of the works of L. Ron Hubbard, who developed *Scientology*®
applied religious philosophy. It is presented to the reader as a record of
observations and research into the nature of the human mind and spirit, and not as
a statement of claims made by the author. The benefits and goals of Scientology
philosophy can be attained only by the dedicated efforts of the reader.

The Purification program cannot be construed as a recommendation of medical
treatment or medication and it is not professed as a physical handling for bodies
nor is any claim made to that effect. There are no medical recommendations or
claims for the Purification program or for any of the vitamin or mineral regimens
described in this book.

No individual should undertake the Purification program or any of its regimens
without first consulting and obtaining the informed approval of a licensed medical
practitioner. The author makes no warranties or representation as to the
effectiveness of the Purification program.

Printed in Denmark by
NEW ERA Publications International ApS

Important Note

In reading this book, be very certain you never go past a word you do not fully understand.

The only reason a person gives up a study or becomes confused or unable to learn is because he or she has gone past a word that was not understood.

The confusion or inability to grasp or learn comes AFTER a word that the person did not have defined and understood.

Have you ever had the experience of coming to the end of a page and realizing you didn't know what you had read? Well, somewhere earlier on that page you went past a word that you had no definition for or an incorrect definition for.

Here's an example. "It was found that when the crepuscule arrived the children were quieter and when it was not present, they were much livelier." You see what happens. You think you don't understand the whole idea, but the inability to understand came entirely from the one word you could not define, *crepuscule*, which means twilight or darkness.

It may not only be the new and unusual words that you will have to look up. Some commonly used words can often be misdefined and so cause confusion.

This datum about not going past an undefined word is the most important fact in the whole subject of study. Every subject you have taken up and abandoned had its words which you failed to get defined.

Therefore, in studying this book be very, very certain you never go past a word you do not fully understand. If the material becomes confusing or you can't seem to grasp it, there will be a word just earlier that you have not understood. Don't go any further, but go back to BEFORE you got into trouble, find the misunderstood word and get it defined.

Definitions

As an aid to the reader, words most likely to be misunderstood have been defined in footnotes the first time they occur in the text. Words sometimes have several meanings. The footnote definitions in this book only give the meaning that the word has as it is used in the text. Other definitions for the word can be found in a dictionary.

A glossary including all the footnote definitions is at the back of this book.

Editors' Foreword

Having realized the potential horrors of the Nuclear Age, L. Ron Hubbard pioneered research into solving the problem of dealing with a new technology which, in the flash of a few short years, had leaped far beyond the capabilities of social and political institutions to harness and control it.

His initial inquiries into the problem of radiation provided a profound look at the real threat to the individual in a society where governments had irrationally involved themselves and their citizens in a nuclear arms race. These findings were released in collaboration with a prominent medical doctor in the first edition of *All About Radiation*.

Further work by Mr. Hubbard yielded a breakthrough in 1979 called the Purification™ program. While researching a way to dislodge the residuals of drugs and other toxins in the body, he developed a precise system of detoxification which was acclaimed to lessen the effects of accumulated radiation. Since then, this program has been completed by tens of thousands of people who report increased energy level, improved perception and a new outlook on life as a result.

The Purification program is vital technology for this day and age, and this new edition of *All About Radiation* has been updated to include a chapter describing its development and application. This edition also includes a new introduction, written by a medical doctor who participated in the scientific studies of the Purification program and the documentation of its results.

We are pleased to present to you this comprehensive work on one of the most important issues of our times—L. Ron Hubbard's *All About Radiation*.

—The Editors, 1989

To those who will not die

*because they **know.***

*"Man's inhumanity to man
makes countless
thousands mourn."*

—Robert Burns

Contents

Introduction

Introduction

Radiation and the Environment

by Gene Denk
Bachelor of Science, Doctor of Medicine

What *is* radiation?

Radiation is defined in the *Random House Dictionary of the English Language* as "a. the process in which energy is emitted as particles or waves; b. the complete process in which energy is emitted by one body, transmitted through an intervening medium or space, and absorbed by another body; c. the energy transferred by these processes."

As a word, *radiation* comes from the Latin *radiatio*, which means "a glittering or shining."

Radiation surrounds us daily. Without it, this page couldn't be seen. Indeed there would be no life on Earth, for sunlight is a type of radiation.

Although unseen, radiation can be measured. One unit of measurement is the *curie*,[1] named after the discoverer of radium

---

1. **curie:** a unit of measurement of radiation. The curie is a representation of how fast a piece of radioactive material disintegrates. Radioactivity is generated by the disintegration of the atoms in an unstable element. One curie of radioactivity is defined as 37 billion disintegrations per second. The curie measures the amount of radioactive material from the viewpoint of how much action is going on in it. There are also other ways of measuring the amount of radiation or the amount of effect radiation has on a given substance.

(a radioactive[2] chemical element,[3] sometimes used on the dials of watches to make them glow in the dark).

There are many sources of radiation in our current society. Some of these are:

1. Nuclear[4] explosions (and fallout[5] from them).

2. Nuclear reactors[6] and the accidents which have occurred with them, releasing radioactive materials.

3. Improper storage or handling of radioactive materials or wastes.

4. The sun, as solar energy. The thinning of the upper atmosphere due to air pollution is progressively letting in more and more radiation from the sun.

5. Radioactive forms of elements which are used in medical diagnostic and therapeutic regimens. The use of these materials has increased considerably over the last twenty years.

---

2. **radioactive:** giving off, or capable of giving off, radiant energy in the form of particles or rays by the spontaneous disintegration of atomic nuclei: said of certain elements, as plutonium, uranium, etc., and their products.

3. **element:** any substance that cannot be separated into different substances by ordinary chemical methods; all matter is composed of such substances. Elements can be transformed into other elements by radioactive decay or by nuclear reactions.

4. **nuclear:** of, characterized by, or operated by the use of atomic energy.

5. **fallout:** the descent to earth of radioactive particles, as after a nuclear explosion or reactor accident; also the radioactive particles themselves.

6. **nuclear reactors:** apparatuses in which an atomic fission chain reaction can be initiated, sustained and controlled, for generating heat or producing useful radiation.

6.   X-rays,[7] either in the treatment of cancerous conditions or in diagnosis.

7.   Radioactive materials occurring naturally in soils and rocks.

To take one example from this list, it was estimated that during the year of 1970 the total amount of radioactive material released into the air and water by nuclear power reactors and processing plants alone over the entire world came to 17 million curies. Compared to 40–80 million created by cosmic rays (high-energy particles which travel across the vast distances of outer space and penetrate our atmosphere), spread out across an entire planet, it did not amount to much. (Of course, if one happened to live near or downwind from a nuclear plant, the dosage would be more concentrated.)

By 1980 the estimated total curies released per year was up to 204 million, with 40–80 million still occurring due to cosmic rays. There is still plenty of air to dilute this but the total amount of radiation is going up rapidly and the effects of extended low-level exposure are not well known. Some experts say there is no safe low level.

A nuclear reactor produces heat through a slow, controlled chain reaction. The chain reaction is produced through an un-stable element (such as uranium[8]) which is decaying by emitting

---

7. **X-rays:** a form of radiation similar to light but of a shorter wavelength and capable of penetrating solids; used in medicine for study, diagnosis and treatment of certain organic disorders, especially of internal structures of the body.

8. **uranium:** a very hard, heavy, silvery radioactive metallic chemical element: It is found only in combination, chiefly in pitchblende (a brown to black lustrous mineral), and is important in work on atomic energy.

subatomic[9] particles (neutrons[10]). These neutrons hit other uranium atoms[11] which cause these atoms to split and release more neutrons. Each neutron can hit another uranium atom and release two more neutrons, each of which can hit another atom. This is the "chain reaction," as the splitting and releasing doubles and redoubles. If not controlled, the result is an explosion. If controlled, the result is heat and very intense radiation. The amount of radiation and heat is proportional to the speed of the reaction.

Despite the proliferation of reactor plants and the increasing sophistication of their safety systems, there is a very small margin for error in the operation of any nuclear reactor. The accidents that have occurred in the past were mainly the result of the reaction getting out of control.

The speed with which a reaction *can* go out of control was shown in an Atomic Energy Commission test that was run in the 1960s. A tiny reactor with a core that was only 15 by 24 inches was allowed to run away to see what would happen. In less than a second, the core soared from 0 to 2.5 billion watts and destroyed itself, demonstrating that there is almost no room for error.

Because there are many safety devices and procedures in reactors to prevent this ultimate reactor catastrophe—and because of luck—there has not been a full-scale meltdown.[12] There

---

9. **subatomic:** of or pertaining to the inner part of an atom or to a particle smaller than an atom.

10. **neutrons:** one of the particles that make up the nucleus of an atom. A neutron has no electrical charge.

11. **atoms:** the smallest components of an element having the chemical properties of that element. It comes from the Greek word *atomos,* undivided.

12. **meltdown:** a situation in which a rapid rise in the power level of a nuclear reactor, as from a defect in the cooling system, results in the melting of the fuel rods and the release of dangerous radiation and may cause the core to sink into the earth.

have, however, been several smaller disasters.

In 1951 a small experimental reactor in Chalk River, Canada, with an extremely safe design, had a partial meltdown due to a small human error that snowballed: the reactor energy output doubled every 2 seconds. The radiation was contained, but a very expensive and long cleanup effort was necessary. Cleanup of an accident is especially difficult because in a very radioactive area workers can only work for a short time and then have to leave as radiation dosage is cumulative. (The human body can only absorb so much radiation during a given period of time before the risk to the person's present and future health becomes too great. Once a worker in a nuclear facility is exposed to this amount of radiation, additional exposure cannot be allowed for a specific amount of time. The amount of time varies with the level of exposure and can be as great as the remainder of the person's lifetime.)

In 1955 a small experimental breeder reactor[13] ran away during a low-power test and a partial meltdown occurred. The secondary safety system worked, but it came very close to an explosion. This reactor doubled its power every 0.2 seconds.

At Windscale[14] (Great Britain) there was an accident in 1957. Uranium in the reactor caught fire. While much of the radioactivity was contained by filters in the structure of the plant, radiation was detected in London, 300 miles away. The plant

---

13. **breeder reactor:** a nuclear reactor generating atomic energy and creating additional fuel by producing more fissionable material than it consumes.

14. **Windscale:** the name and location of a nuclear plant (now called Sellafield) in England, 300 miles northwest of London, where in 1957 a uranium fuel element burst, causing a uranium fire and a major release of radiation into the atmosphere. Fallout from the accident was measured in Ireland, London, Mol (Belgium) and Frankfurt.

became unusable and had to be sealed and written off. Great quantities of agricultural products in the surrounding communities had to be destroyed as a result of contamination.

In 1958 there was another accident at Chalk River with a different reactor. Broken hardware resulted in a piece of a damaged fuel rod[15] catching fire.

In 1961 an experimental reactor in Idaho, called SL-1, designed to produce only 200 kilowatts of power, killed three men, apparently due to one control rod[16] being pulled too far out momentarily. Enormous amounts of radiation were released into the reactor building but not much escaped to the environment.

In the Enrico Fermi reactor outside Detroit, Michigan in 1966, a small piece of metal blocked one of the cooling inlets for the liquid sodium coolant it used, and part of the fuel assembly melted during testing. The reactor had to be dismantled at great expense over a period of time and taken away in pieces to be disposed of as radioactive waste.

More recently in 1979 at Three Mile Island[17] near Harrisburg, Pennsylvania in the US, a minor hardware failure and operator errors resulted in a partial meltdown and a cleanup effort that went on for years, including the disposal of 700,000 gallons of radioactive water.

---

15. **fuel rod:** nuclear fuel contained in a long thin-walled tube; an array of such tubes forming the core of a nuclear reactor.

16. **control rod:** a neutron-absorbing material in the shape of a rod or other arrangement of parts, that can be moved into or out of the core of a nuclear reactor to regulate the rate of fission.

17. **Three Mile Island:** the location of a reactor facility outside Harrisburg, Pennsylvania, where in March, 1979 a series of human and equipment failures caused a significant meltdown of nuclear fuel and the escape of a cloud of radioactive gas.

In April 1986 the Chernobyl[18] nuclear plant in the Soviet Union, with a similar design to Windscale, caught fire and destroyed part of the reactor building, releasing radioactive material which was carried by the wind over Poland and into Europe and Scandinavia, to say nothing of the Soviet Union itself. It may have done at least a partial meltdown.

In a study done by the Atomic Energy Commission in 1957, it was estimated that the radiation from a major accident at a small (by present standards) nuclear power reactor would kill 3,400 people up to 15 miles away, give severe radiation sickness[19] to 43,000 people up to 44 miles away, double the chance of cancer in people up to 200 miles away (182,000 people at 1957 population density) and cause 7 billion dollars worth of property damage (at 1957 rates). A full-size accident in one of today's much larger plants would be much worse.

There are other hazards in dealing with reactors. What does one do with damaged reactor parts and other radioactive wastes, and how does one "decommission" a reactor when it is no longer usable?

The constant bombardment of the components of the reactor makes its parts very radioactive. One cannot simply walk in and cut it apart. Some of the radioactive materials in the reactor remain radioactive for tens of thousands of years.

---

18. **Chernobyl:** a city in the USSR, site of a nuclear reactor plant where, in late April 1986, systems malfunctioned causing an explosion of one of the reactor buildings and a fire of a reactor core. Radiation contamination from this accident spread across much of the western USSR as well as eastern and central Europe and Scandinavia.

19. **radiation sickness:** sickness caused by irradiation with X-rays or other nuclear radiation as a result of therapeutic treatment, accidental exposure, or a nuclear bomb explosion and characterized by nausea, vomiting, headache, cramps, diarrhea, loss of hair and teeth, destruction of white blood cells, and prolonged hemorrhage.

Processing uranium and other nuclear fuels produces large amounts of radioactive liquids which can't just be poured down a drain. These must be sealed and transported to where they can safely reside for the next 200,000 years. The problem is that there is no container known that will last for 200,000 years. Some radioactive waste was put in barrels and dumped in the ocean and the barrels are now breaking down and allowing the waste to leak. Other containers of radioactive waste were put into salt mines, but heat given off by these materials softens the salt formations, thus making it possible for the containers to sink into the salt or otherwise shift around. This makes future removal of the material from such a site doubtful and increases the risk of the radioactivity leaking into the environment.

In short, the technology of how to safely handle the disposal of radioactive waste has not caught up with the technology of how to create it. In fact, it is not even close.

Occasionally radioactive material is accidentally spilled into the environment, such as a river for example. Some of the radiation gets recovered, and some of it goes out and makes the world just a little more radioactive.

It is estimated that if trends continue, by the year 2000 the radiation exposure a person receives from artificial sources of radiation will be twice that of natural radiation sources.

Another source of radiation, and the most dangerous, is atomic weapons. There have been 1,525 known nuclear bomb tests. The fallout from atmospheric tests was at its highest in 1963 when it added 7 percent to our radiation dosage from natural sources. This has decreased to less than 1 percent now, and most nuclear tests are conducted underground, where little radiation escapes into the atmosphere.

The case of Bikini[20] atoll[21] in the South Pacific gives us some actual experience with the effects of fallout from nuclear weapons. Twenty three nuclear device tests were detonated on Bikini between 1946 and 1958. One of these was a 15-megaton[22] hydrogen bomb[23] test called Bravo.

While the natives were evacuated to other islands, unexpected wind changes during nuclear tests sent fallout over their relocation sites. Some of these people died, many contracted various illnesses, including leukemia[24] or other cancers, years after exposure to radiation.

It has been estimated that it should be safe to return to Bikini in another 90 years. By that time, the Bikini islanders will have waited 130 years to return to their home.

The above is a very broad look at radiation across the face of the world. What about closer to home?

Individuals in all walks of life are exposed daily to varying degrees of radiation.

---

20. **Bikini:** an island in the Pacific where atomic bomb tests were conducted in 1946.

21. **atoll:** a ring-shaped coral island nearly or completely surrounding a lagoon.

22. **megaton:** the explosive force of a million tons of TNT. A 15-megaton bomb is the equivalent of 15 million tons of TNT.

23. **hydrogen bomb:** a bomb, more powerful than an atomic bomb, that derives its explosive energy from the thermonuclear fusion reaction of certain forms of hydrogen.

24. **leukemia:** any of several cancers of the bone marrow that prevent the normal manufacture of red and white blood cells and platelets (the minute bodies in the blood that aid in coagulation), resulting in anemia, increased susceptibility to infection and impaired blood clotting.

The use of X-rays in medicine, sunbathing or tanning under ultraviolet[25] lights are just a few sources of exposure.

These are all relatively minor. However, the factor to bear in mind is that radiation is accumulative.

What exactly does radiation *do* to a human body?

Radiation is produced by the breakdown of unstable dense atoms into less dense atoms with the release of particles or waves of energy. These particles/waves have high energy characteristics and can pass directly through the body when it is in close proximity to a nuclear incident or when taken into the body as a result of contamination of the air, water and food by fallout of radioactive materials. Radioactive elements emit different forms of particles or waves. These elements can be absorbed into the body through the lungs, intestines and skin.

As radiation passes through the body or when a radioactive substance is incorporated into specific tissues, it transfers its high-energy state to the exposed body systems. As the energy is passed from the radioactive particle to the surrounding cells and body fluids, it agitates the atoms and molecules[26] making up the body. This transfer of energy leads to cellular disruption, damage or even death, depending on the dosage of radiation received and the physical health of the individual at the time of exposure.

---

25. **ultraviolet:** pertaining to a band of radiation having wavelengths that are shorter than violet light.

26. **molecules:** the smallest particles of an element or compound that can exist in the free state and still retain the characteristics of the element or compound: the molecules of elements consist of one atom or two or more similar atoms; those of compounds consist of two or more different atoms.

Radiation increases (detrimentally) the activity of all biological systems. The basic elements that make up the body are carbon, oxygen, nitrogen and sulfur. Oxygen plays a central role in breaking down carbohydrates[27] and fats into energy. This fuels the cells and makes possible the production of proteins which are vital in giving form and substance to the body. Oxygen is also key in the production of enzymes[28] which catalyze[29] biochemical[30] reactions.

When radiation strikes an atom or molecule in the body, it can cause an electron[31] to be released. Free electrons are generally taken up by an oxygen molecule. Having an extra electron, this oxygen molecule is unstable; it has a tendency to react with other molecules. It will tend to pull an electron from another nearby molecule in order to restabilize itself. The molecule this additional electron is taken from is now in an unstable state and will pull an electron from yet another molecule. The result is an actual chain reaction occurring in the body. Thus, reactive oxygen molecules disrupt cellular function and structure.

Since oxygen is found inside and outside the cells in large quantities, the production of large amounts of reactive oxygen by radiation exposure will lead to the disruption of other compounds in cells as these molecules attempt to restabilize.

---

27. **carbohydrates:** organic compounds, such as sugars and starches, composed of carbon, oxygen and hydrogen. Carbohydrates are an important class of foods in animal nutrition, supplying energy to the body.

28. **enzymes:** complex organic substances secreted by certain cells of plants and animals which cause a chemical change in the substance upon which they act.

29. **catalyze:** to cause or accelerate a chemical change without the substance causing the change being affected.

30. **biochemical:** relating to the chemical substances occurring in living organisms.

31. **electron:** a negatively charged particle that forms a part of all atoms, and can exist on its own in a free state.

The affected substances in the body can be fats or proteins, which are vital to the normal function of cells. If certain proteins found in the cell are affected it can lead to mutation effects which can in turn predispose the body to cancer.

Thus, radiation produces a burst of free electrons in the body. This then produces reactive oxygen and other transformed materials which rip and tear into tissues causing:

1. disruption of cell structure

2. suppression of enzyme activity

3. formation of abnormal proteins

4. formation of mutation-causing and cancer-forming substances

5. death of cells.

The human body does have defenses against the effect radiation brings about within it. Antioxidants are such a defense. Antioxidants are inhibitors, substances which operate in the body to slow down or hinder a chemical reaction.

As covered above, reactive oxygen disrupts cellular function by a type of chain reaction. The body produces only small amounts of reactive oxygen in its normal day-to-day function, but this is normally removed and detoxified[32] by the body's own control system for handling such substances: antioxidants. If the body did not have such a control system it could not survive.

---

32. **detoxified:** changed (toxins) into less toxic or more readily excretable substances.

Types of antioxidants used by the body include vitamin C,[33] vitamin E,[34] vitamin A[35] and various enzymes. These substances are normally obtained through a healthy, balanced diet. They can also be obtained through vitamin supplements commonly available.

From this it can be reasoned that an adequately nourished individual whose tissues are well saturated with these nutrients will be less likely to be the victim of an assault on the natural structure of the body's tissues and cells by reactive compounds created by radiation.

Over the last century, man has been exposing himself to an ever-increasing number of chemical compounds which are foreign to living systems. They are capable of causing chemical breakdowns, the products of which can impair or disrupt cell function and even cause the death of cells. Such compounds include:

1.   toxic[36] gases formed from industrial waste products reacting with the atmosphere (nitrogen dioxide,[37] ozone,[38]

---

33. **vitamin C:** also called ascorbic acid; a colorless, crystalline, water-soluble vitamin, found in many foods, especially citrus fruits, vegetables and rose hips and also made synthetically; it is required for proper nutrition and metabolism.

34. **vitamin E:** a vitamin important in keeping oxygen from combining with waste products to form toxic compounds, and in red blood cell health.

35. **vitamin A:** a vitamin important in bone growth, healthy skin, sexual function and reproduction.

36. **toxic:** acting as or having the effect of a poison, poisonous.

37. **nitrogen dioxide:** a highly toxic brownish gas, used as an industrial chemical and also released as an air pollutant during the burning of fossil fuels such as coal, oil or natural gas.

38. **ozone:** a form of oxygen with a sharp odor, produced by electricity and present in the air, especially after a thunderstorm. It is also one of the toxic pollutants present in smog.

sulfur dioxide[39] and others)

2. toxic metals (mercury,[40] nickel,[41] arsenic[42] and cadmium[43])

3. toxic chemicals found in solvents and pesticides (the number of these is profuse; a few of these are acetaldehyde,[44] formaldehyde,[45] carbon tetrachloride,[46] benzene,[47] chlordane,[48] heptachlor[49] and toluene[50])

---

39. **sulfur dioxide:** a colorless, nonflammable, suffocating gas, formed when sulfur burns; used chiefly in the manufacture of chemicals such as sulfuric acid, in preserving fruits and vegetables, and in bleaching, disinfecting and fumigating.

40. **mercury:** a heavy, silver white metallic element that is liquid at ordinary temperatures; quicksilver. Ingestion of mercury (for example, by eating fish caught in polluted waters) can damage the central nervous system, causing tremors and poor coordination and, in severe cases, brain damage.

41. **nickel:** a hard, silvery white metallic element, much used as an alloy and in electroplating. Certain forms of nickel are toxic when inhaled into the body as dust.

42. **arsenic:** a silvery white, brittle, very poisonous chemical element, compounds of which are used in making insecticides, glass, medicines, etc.

43. **cadmium:** a silver white metallic chemical element found in zinc ores. It is used in some low-melting alloys, electroplating, rechargeable batteries, etc. It has highly toxic dust or fumes.

44. **acetaldehyde:** a colorless, flammable liquid used as a solvent.

45. **formaldehyde:** a colorless, toxic gas, having a suffocating odor: used chiefly as a disinfectant and preservative. It has been linked to forms of cancer and is toxic to the central nervous system.

46. **carbon tetrachloride:** a colorless, nonflammable liquid, often used in fire extinguishers and in cleaning fluids. Its fumes are very dangerous if inhaled.

47. **benzene:** a colorless, flammable liquid obtained chiefly from coal tar. It is used for removing grease stains and in making dyes and synthetic rubber. Benzene can cause leukemia and chromosome damage in people exposed to it.

48. **chlordane:** a highly poisonous, volatile oil, formerly used as an insecticide.

49. **heptachlor:** a waxy solid, formerly used as an insecticide.

50. **toluene:** a colorless, flammable, aromatic liquid obtained from coal tar and petroleum and used as a solvent and for making explosives, dyes, etc.

---

4.   drugs, such as tranquilizers, cocaine,[51] marijuana,[52] psychiatric drugs, etc.

Exposure to these substances puts an additional strain on the body's antioxidant reserves and can cause their depletion.

So there are two major risk factors that predispose a human body to damage by radiation:

1.   exposure to environmental pollutants and drugs

2.   low antioxidant reserves due to poor diet and/or high individual need.

Thus it will be those individuals whose bodies are poorly nourished and exposed to chemical pollutants and drugs who will be most susceptible to harmful effects from exposure to radiation.

Until now, there appeared to be no solution to the problem of radiation. However, it appears possible to "proof up" the body so that it is not so susceptible to damage. Research has shown this to be possible by maintaining a nutrient-rich, additive-free diet and by supplementing the diet with antioxidant-rich nutrients. By taking these simple steps the antioxidant "arsenal" can be built up to readiness to cope with any additional stresses that may be imposed on it.

An apparently very effective way to proof up the body against possible future stress is by reducing the foreign chemical load already stored in the body. It was discovered by L. Ron Hubbard that many toxic substances can accumulate in the fatty

51. **cocaine:** a bitter, crystalline drug obtained from the dried leaves of the coca shrub; it is a local anesthetic and a dangerous, illegal stimulant.

52. **marijuana:** the dried leaves and flowers of the hemp plant, used in cigarette form as a narcotic or hallucinogen.

tissues of the body, which then act as a reservoir for these destructive substances. They can "leak out" and cause damage to other tissues and also deplete antioxidant reserves. By unburdening the body of these toxic chemical stores, it could well be that an individual would be more able to withstand the adverse effects of radiation or toxic chemical exposure.

How would one be able to remove accumulated chemical toxins from the body? There is only one method in existence for doing this which has been rigorously tested and found effective—the Purification program developed by L. Ron Hubbard. This is a highly precise regimen involving the use of exercise, various nutritional supplements including niacin[53] (which is a powerful mobilizer of chemicals accumulated in the body), prescribed periods of time in a sauna, a well-balanced diet and a well-ordered schedule which provides adequate rest.

In fact, the proper use of this program has resulted in documented reductions of pesticides and other persistent toxic chemicals from body fat and tissues.

Additionally, niacin itself appears to be beneficial in removing the effects of prior radiation exposure. Extensive research has been conducted in this field by L. Ron Hubbard, as he describes in this book.

Effective chemical detoxification therefore gives us hope that not only can the effects of radiation be reduced, but that resistance to further exposure can be increased. This is a welcome light shed on a field so long plagued by the lack of any real

---

53. **niacin:** a white, odorless, crystalline substance found in protein foods or prepared synthetically. It is a member of the vitamin B complex. *See also* **vitamin B complex** in the glossary.

remedies for the seemingly irreversible damage that radiation can cause.

Dr. Denk graduated Bachelor of Science from University of Michigan and Doctor of Medicine at University of Washington at Seattle. He maintains a private practice in Los Angeles and has participated in independent scientific studies of L. Ron Hubbard's Purification program.

Book One

The Facts About the Atomic Bomb

by Farley R. Spink

Master of Arts
Bachelor of Medicine
Bachelor of Surgery

Book One
Chapter One

The Atomic Bomb

Let it be stated definitely at the outset that a thing understood is a thing less feared. Atomic energy in all its uses has been the subject of much mystery and secrecy. This is so partly because the peculiarly "atomic" radiations are imperceptible to human senses and partly on account of national security measures. Some clarity needs to be brought at once into the public attitude regarding atomic weapons and it is hoped that the following simple explanations of both what man is facing and what he can do to help himself, may achieve this.

The so-called "nominal bomb" will be the main subject of description. This is roughly equivalent in power to 20,000 tons of conventional high explosive (TNT[1]) and is described therefore as a 20-kiloton[2] (20 kt) bomb. The weapons used on Japan in 1945 were of this order of magnitude. The hydrogen, or thermonuclear,[3] weapon differs in its effects from the above only in

---

1. **TNT:** a high explosive unaffected by ordinary friction or shock: used chiefly in military and other explosive devices. TNT is short for *trinitrotoluene.*
2. **kiloton:** an explosive force equal to that of 1,000 tons of TNT.
3. **thermonuclear:** of, pertaining to or involving the nuclear fusion reaction that takes place between the nuclei of a gas, especially hydrogen, heated to a temperature of several million degrees.

quantity, not in quality. A brief reference will be made in a later paragraph to the important differences and the special dangers.

The mechanism of the bomb is basically simple and a slight understanding of it is useful to trace the development of its action. The explosive material is a pure mass of fissionable[4] metal. A form of uranium and plutonium[5] were the first such materials to be discovered. The only other fundamental constituent[6] required is a source of neutrons (uncharged subatomic particles).

Atoms of the metal can capture wandering neutrons. The nucleus[7] of the atom thus augmented is unstable and immediately splits into two roughly equal halves which form the nuclei[8] of lighter elements (the "fission[9] products"). At the same time two neutrons are released for each one captured and each atom of metal split. These may escape from the bomb mass or may be captured by more atoms of metal. If the total mass is greater than a certain critical size, more neutrons are captured than escape and a chain reaction develops. It proceeds in a bomb at an enormous rate (10^{12} stages in one second) and at each stage, much energy is liberated.[10] Much of it is in the form of heat and at the point of explosion, a temperature of a million degrees centigrade is produced almost instantaneously, rendering the air and the remains of the bomb incandescent.[11] This is the fireball which radiates a tremendous flash of heat and light, and the

---

4. **fissionable:** capable of or possessing a nucleus or nuclei capable of undergoing fission. *See also* **fission** below.
5. **plutonium:** a radioactive chemical element, used in nuclear weapons and reactors.
6. **constituent:** an element of which something is composed or made up; component.
7. **nucleus:** the central part of an atom, composed of protons and neutrons and making up almost all of the mass of the atom: it carries a positive charge.
8. **nuclei:** plural of **nucleus**.
9. **fission:** the act of cleaving or splitting into parts. *Nuclear fission* is the splitting of the nucleus of an atom into nuclei of lighter atoms, accompanied by the release of energy. The word comes from Latin *fission,* meaning "a splitting, dividing."
10. **liberated:** disengaged; set free from combination.
11. **incandescent:** glowing or white with heat.

very high pressure (½ million tons per sq. in.) suddenly created within it sets up the blast wave.

Part of the energy is released at the same time as the highly penetrating, invisible gamma rays.[12] A large quantity of neutrons is, of course, also released and is the other important invisible component of the radiation. These last two factors are highly dangerous to life and constitute the one fundamental respect in which atomic explosions differ from the conventional.

The fireball, which is about 450 yards in diameter, expands and rises rapidly into the upper atmosphere to become the familiar mushroom-shaped cloud. The light flash lasts for an instant only, the heat radiation for, at most, half a second, and the blast passes in a single wave taking perhaps one second. Most of the gamma and neutron radiation has passed in a couple of seconds, but some continues for about a minute, in fact until the radio-active cloud has risen into the upper atmosphere out of range.

Of all the effects of an atomic explosion the most important by far is blast. This of course is nothing new. Anyone who has been involved in war has had plenty of experience of it. It will inevitably cause an enormous amount of material damage and was in fact, in Japan, responsible for 60 percent of the casualties.

The heat flash is the next most important, causing directly or indirectly 25 percent of the casualties.

The invisible nuclear radiation caused only 15 percent of the casualties. In terms of a single bomb explosion, these are thus rather a minor consideration. They are, however, much feared

---

12. **gamma rays:** radiations which are similar to X-rays, but with a shorter wavelength than X-rays. Because of their short wavelength, gamma rays are very penetrating. They have a range in air of about 1½ miles and are the principal cause of radiation disease in atomic warfare.

partly on account of their very invisibility and have been the subject of much controversial discussion. Breaking the new effects down numerically in this fashion tends to impart a real sense of proportion on the matter.

The real danger to life on a planetary scale does not lie in these immediate radiations. Here is the point. The explosion of the bomb produces a considerable amount of breakdown products, called fission products, by the splitting of the atoms of uranium. These are all initially radioactive and contaminate the atmosphere, settling gradually to earth as dust over a period of years. Some of the products retain their radioactivity for more than twenty years so that an accumulation is bound to occur. The explosion of bombs for any purpose, military or otherwise, even at quite long intervals, can only increase the general radioactivity of Earth and atmosphere towards the danger point.

On account of the slow subsidence of dust from the upper atmosphere the actual effect would probably be postponed although inevitable. It has also been suggested that the explosion of about one thousand H-bombs altogether might be enough to destroy all life on the planet. If this figure should be inaccurate by a factor as great as ten, the situation is one which demands the urgent attention of every human being.

One other matter remains for inclusion in these general considerations. The psychological effect of an atomic explosion is considerable and interesting. Any person suffering a sudden and severe shock tends to go into a temporary state of helpless apathy. The duration of this state and its intensity, however, do vary a great deal according to the basic mental stability of the persons concerned. The atomic explosion is an instantaneous and utterly overwhelming shock, of a magnitude hitherto unknown on Earth. It produces in surviving victims a state of apathy of extraordinary degree. It is stated that, after the

Japanese incidents, for a full twenty minutes following the explosion, no attempt was made by anyone to do anything. The reader will perceive that this is likely to produce a permanent effect on an individual's mentality. There is some evidence also that the invisible nuclear radiations already referred to can themselves directly affect the mind. The possibility of wholesale mental aberration[13] resulting from either of these causes in atomic warfare is one which cannot be lightly ignored. The reader is invited to ponder on this.

---

13. **aberration:** a departure from rational thought or behavior. It means basically to err, to make mistakes, or more specifically to have fixed ideas which are not true. The word is also used in its scientific sense. It means departure from a straight line. If a line should go from A to B and it is *aberrated*, it would go from A to some other point, to some other point, to some other point, to some other point, to some other point, and finally arrive at B. Taken in its scientific sense, it would also mean the lack of straightness or to see crookedly as, in example, a man sees a horse but thinks he sees an elephant. Aberrated conduct would be wrong conduct, or conduct not supported by reason. Aberration is opposed to sanity, which would be its opposite. From the Latin, *aberrare*, to wander from; Latin, *ab*, away, *errare*, to wander.

Book One
Chapter Two

Protection

**Book One
Chapter Two**

Protection

Blast

The blast from an atomic weapon differs somewhat in character from that experienced with conventional high explosives. The latter type of explosion gives a very short, sharp blow lasting not more than a hundredth of a second, followed by an opposite phase of suction lasting perhaps twice as long. It happens in practice that the suction phase does the most damage, i.e., walls tend to fall outwards. The nuclear bomb, in contrast, gives a positive push lasting about one second. That is to say, it resembles a very strong wind. Most of the damage is done during this positive phase of the blast wave. Walls and buildings are pushed away from the point of explosion. Here is in fact a definite resemblance to the type of damage caused by natural storms. The suction phase is relatively unimportant.

The range of the blast wave and the degrees of damage that might be expected will now be described briefly.

Ordinary houses would be completely collapsed to a range of one thousand yards from ground zero. (*Ground zero* is the term used to describe the point on the ground immediately beneath the bomb when it explodes.) Up to a mile from ground zero irreparable damage could be expected. At greater distances, houses would be rendered uninhabitable until major repairs had been done (1½ miles) or first aid (2½ miles). More lightly constructed buildings would, of course, be severely damaged or destroyed at even greater distances, say, up to a mile and a half. Reinforced concrete on the other hand, would probably survive outside a 600-yard radius with no more than superficial damage.

A major problem arising from blast would be the tremendous amount of debris blocking streets. This did not arise particularly in Japan, since the houses were mostly wooden and were completely destroyed by fire. But in a Western city complete impassability would be likely for a distance of half a mile or more from ground zero. Severe hampering of fire fighting and rescue work would inevitably result.

As regards the effect of blast on personnel, there would be few direct casualties. Anyone close enough to the explosion to be killed by blast would be killed anyway by the other factors. However, many casualties would be expected due to collapsing buildings at various ranges.

Protection of personnel from blast can be achieved to a degree by similar measures to those familiar in "conventional" warfare. Deep shelters and basements with several means of exit should be satisfactory against anything but a ground-level burst close by. The "Anderson" type shelter[1] much used in the 1939–45 war, or a deep trench with a thick layer of earth on top, provides fair protection. No particularly new problem exists here. The difference between an atomic weapon and an H-bomb is a matter only of size.

---

1. **"Anderson" type shelter:** a small prefabricated air-raid shelter devised by William Paterson, a Scottish engineer, and adopted while Sir John Anderson was the British Home Secretary (1930–40). Anderson shelters were used in Britain during World War II. They were curved, steel huts which some people buried in their gardens and covered with 2 or 3 feet of earth to protect them from the effects of explosion.

The blast wave travels at about the speed of sound. That is to say, it does not arrive at a point a mile or two from the explosion center for several seconds after the light flash. There is, therefore, time to dive for cover, and this gives a slight safety factor. By the same means, some of the gamma radiation may be escaped and, in the case of a hydrogen bomb, some of the heat as well.

The basic principles amount, therefore, to "Take cover if you can" and, where more time is available, "Go underground."

Heat

The heat flash radiating in straight lines outward from the fireball lasts in its full intensity for only a fraction of a second. On account of the short duration only the surfaces of objects are affected. At these surfaces, however, a temperature of several thousand degrees centigrade is reached, up to a range of ½–¾ mile. Within this distance surfaces of granite[2] are melted and on humans exposed in the open, burns involving the whole skin thickness are to be expected with some internal damage and immediate death. Since the flash is brief and nonpenetrating, relatively slight protection is a considerable safeguard. Any person properly under cover, i.e., out of the direct path of the rays, would not be affected. Clothing, particularly if loose, woolen and of a light color, offers appreciable[3] protection, although the clothing itself might catch fire. Severe to moderate burns would be suffered up to 1½–2 miles and slight burns at a greater distance.

The risk of fires and resulting burns is, of course, great. Combustible materials like cloth, dry wood, paper, etc., may well be ignited up to a distance of 1½ miles. This can occur inside

---

2. **granite:** a hard, coarse-grained rock, much used for buildings and monuments.
3. **appreciable:** sufficient to be readily perceived or estimated; considerable.

buildings if the heat flash can enter through windows, open doors, etc. A simple means of protection for brick buildings is obvious: any kind of white opaque screen or even simply white-washing windows would confer an appreciable degree of safety.

Fires arising from other causes constitute an additional danger. Damage to gas mains, overturning of domestic heating equipment of any kind and scattering of burning debris are more familiar wartime phenomena and no less important here.

There is a peculiarity in the manner of healing of burns caused by atomic explosions. This is a pronounced tendency to form thick, knotted, overgrown scars, known as keloids, which are very disfiguring and may be crippling. They were observed in Japan, and may be the result of the action of burning plus radiation. Malnutrition and poor treatment do definitely contribute, however; these were pronounced factors in Hiroshima[4] and Nagasaki.[5] Treatment, once keloids have developed, lies in the field of plastic surgery.

Light flash

As previously described a tremendous flash of light radiates for an instant at the moment of explosion. Its intensity, as seen during tests in the Pacific from a distance of 18 miles, was several times greater than that of the sun. Anybody without protection for the eyes would be totally blinded at a distance of several miles but, on past experience, the sight can be expected to recover within a matter of hours. There is some evidence that superficial skin burns due to light flash rather than heat can also occur even a number of miles from ground zero. These are not serious but

---

4. **Hiroshima:** a seaport in southwest Japan; site of the first military use of the atomic bomb on 6 August 1945.
5. **Nagasaki:** a seaport in southwest Japan; site of the second military use of the atomic bomb on 9 August 1945.

can be very unpleasant. They are probably due to the ultraviolet component of the light.

Radiation

Several types of nuclear radiation are released by atomic explosions. These are:

Alpha particles: Helium nuclei, therefore relatively heavy and slow, penetrate a very short distance in air and are of no importance in this context.

Beta particles: Electrons traveling at nearly the speed of light, penetrating a few feet in air, also of no importance in this context.

(Radioactive fission products coming in closer contact with the body can cause considerable damage, however, by means of these radiations, as covered later in this text.)

Gamma rays: These, for practical purposes, are X-rays. They are of the same nature as light but of much higher frequency. They have a range in air of about 1½ miles and are the principal cause of radiation disease in atomic warfare.

Neutrons: These electrically uncharged particles are also more penetrating. They travel a mile or more in air and cause damage to the body. They have the additional property of inducing radioactivity in objects which they strike.

A description of the actual effects of these rays on the human body follows in the next chapter. Meanwhile the problem of protection from them must be considered.

The intensity of gamma rays falls off with increasing distance from the source according to the inverse square law:[6] that is to say, at double the distance the intensity would be reduced to a quarter. This applies to bomb bursts and small sources of radiation but not where the distance is small compared with the dimensions of the radiating surface. They are absorbed to some extent by air which, of course, limits their range, and by mist, fog or smoke rather more effectively. Their intensity is reduced by half by the following thicknesses of common protective substances approximately:

Lead	1"	Concrete	5"
Steel	1½"	Earth	8"
Water	11"		

These figures would be of some value in estimating the effectiveness of various sheltering constructions. The "Anderson" type shelter already referred to would reduce immediate radiation danger at moderate ranges very considerably. However, the thicker and heavier the protection, the better. The radiation from a burst only lasts a few seconds with a much smaller amount over a longer period. This last can, therefore, be escaped, together with the blast, if cover is taken at once when the light flash is seen.

---

6. **inverse square law:** (*physics, optics*) one of several laws relating two quantities such that one quantity varies inversely as the square of the other. There are laws using this basic principle which apply to magnetism, sound and light. An example of this would be that of the illumination produced on a screen by a point source of light: if the distance between the light source and screen were doubled, the illumination on the screen would be reduced to a quarter of its original intensity; if the distance were trebled, the illumination would be reduced to one-ninth; if the distance were quadrupled, the illumination would be reduced to one-sixteenth, etc. Likewise, the intensity of sound decreases as the distance from its source increases: a bell 10 feet away sounds one-fourth as loud as the same bell 5 feet away; and if 15 feet away, it sounds one-ninth as loud as when 5 feet away. Applied to radiation, the *inverse square law* states that the intensity of radiation decreases in proportion to the square of the distance from its source.

Book One
Chapter Three

Nuclear Radiation

Nuclear Radiation

The effects of radiations depend basically on their property of rendering atoms in their path electrically charged. This is called ionization. The immediate result in the molecules, of which the ionized atoms are part, is increased chemical activity and a tendency to break up. Thus the living structure of the cell is altered or destroyed and poisonous waste products may be formed. These changes, if on a sufficiently large scale, and in vital organs, can cause the death of the whole body.

The ionizing power of radiation depends on its energy. Alpha and beta particles are far more effective than gamma rays, but fortunately have very little penetrating power. Neutrons have quite high ionizing power, and penetrate easily as well. Dosages of radiation are measured in terms of total ionization, the unit being the "roentgen"[1](r). It is difficult to gain any subjective appreciation of what is meant by a dose of say 500r, but the following observations give some idea:

The lethal dose for a human being, if received uniformly over the whole body, is about 750r. That is to say, that such a dose could be expected to kill 100 percent of persons exposed to

---

1. **roentgen:** (*physics*) the unit of exposure to X-rays or gamma rays. Whereas a *curie* measures the amount of activity in radioactive material itself, a *roentgen* is a measure of the radiation generated by that material. Named after German physicist Wilhelm Conrad Röntgen (1845–1923) who discovered X-rays in 1895. Abbreviation *r*.

it, and is called an LD_{100}[2] dose. It would be received by a person standing in the open at about 800 yards from ground zero in the case of a nominal bomb blast. An amount of 450r, such as would be received at up to 1,300 yards or so, would kill about 50 percent of persons exposed; it is thus an LD_{50} dose. Less than 200r is not ordinarily fatal, unless the victim is already weakened from some other cause or has received burns or blast injury as well.

About 50 percent of people exposed to a single dose of 200r, however, could become quite ill, and might take anything up to three months to recover. 100r produces about 10 percent sickness only, and less than 50r in one dose can be taken as relatively harmless, provided there is no further exposure for many weeks, at least.

It will be obvious from the above that a good deal of individual variation occurs, but beyond the observation that the very young, the old and the ill are more sensitive than normal, nothing is known of the reasons for the variations.

Much greater amounts of radiation than the above can be tolerated if directed to specific parts of the body only, as for example in radiotherapy[3] for cancer. On the other hand, much smaller doses delivered to the whole body do produce some ill effects, and furthermore, accumulate over a period of time. The sensitivity of human tissues decreases in this order: lymphatic tissue,[4] testes,[5] bone marrow (blood-forming tissue), epithelium (lining) of the stomach and intestines, ovaries.[6] Brain and muscle are the least sensitive of all, and other tissues fall in between the

---

2. **LD:** abbreviation for lethal dose.
3. **radiotherapy:** treatment of diseases by means of X-rays or of radioactive substances.
4. **lymphatic tissue:** tissue in the body which creates or conveys *lymph*, a clear, yellowish fluid containing white blood cells in a liquid resembling blood plasma.
5. **testes:** the male reproductive glands, two oval glands located in the scrotum.
6. **ovaries:** female reproductive glands producing eggs and, in vertebrates, sex hormones.

two ranges. 1000r to brain only is not lethal. On the other hand, 0.2r per day over a period has been known to depress blood formation in workers with X-rays. The maximum safe continuous rate of irradiation[7] for such people is now considered to be about 0.1r per day for five days a week. While a total dose accumulated over a long period is not as dangerous as the same dose given in a short time, radiation effects do nevertheless accumulate. In actual fact, 60r spread over three weeks is no more effective than 20r as a single rapid dose. Nevertheless the expectation of life for radiologists,[8] as observed in the USA, is about five years less than that for others, and the incidence of leukemia in this group may be as high as ten times that in the whole population.

Death from irradiation may occur from several immediate causes, according to the dose received. Huge doses of many thousands of roentgen cause death from brain damage within a few hours. Death from an LD_{100} is usual due to destruction of the intestines and occurs in about 7–10 days. Smaller doses such as an LD_{50} may produce the same effect, or the victim may die from failure of blood manufacture in 4–6 weeks or so. If this period is survived recovery normally occurs, though the chronic risks remain, even with very small doses. Thus a number of victims can be expected to die after years from, for example, leukemia.

The general pattern of radiation disease from a rapid exposure is as follows: The primary symptoms — nausea, diarrhea and particularly vomiting — appear in 2 to 24 hours, and may last 2 to 14 days or so. Secondary symptoms — fever, bleeding under the skin and from orifices,[9] loss of hair and more diarrhea appear

---

7. **irradiation:** exposure or the process of exposure to X-rays or other radiation.
8. **radiologists:** those who deal with X-rays or nuclear radiation, especially for medical uses.
9. **orifices:** openings or apertures which serve as or have the form of a mouth, as of a tube, of the stomach, bladder or other bodily organ, of a wound, etc.; the mouth of any cavity.

after an interval of some few days up to several weeks. The earlier the onset of symptoms of either type and the longer they last, the worse is the outlook for the patient, and an indication is thereby given of the dose received. Loss of hair and bleeding in the first week are the gravest signs; death is certain.

Most of the available data regarding the biological effects of radiation has been derived from observations made in Japan during and since 1945, supplemented by a growing body of evidence from animal experiments. Owing to the obvious impossibility of direct research on human beings, however, the picture is still far from complete.

Book One
Chapter Four

The
Hydrogen Bomb

The Hydrogen Bomb

The H-bomb or thermonuclear weapon will now be described briefly. The explosion is a three-stage process:

1. An "ordinary" atom bomb serves as a "trigger."

2. The high temperature it produces makes possible the fusion[1] of atoms of two rare forms of the element hydrogen. This reaction liberates more energy, and in particular, yields large quantities of neutrons of much higher speeds than occur in the first stage.

3. These produce fission of the common and normally stable atoms of uranium. Large quantities of this can be used, as the casing of the bomb, for example, and the power of the bomb is increased simply by adding more of it.

The power is expressed in terms of equivalence to millions of tons of TNT (megatons). Weapons of up to forty or more megatons have been tested, but the following descriptions will refer to a 10-megaton bomb exploded at ground level.

---

1. **fusion:** the combining of lightweight atomic nuclei into a nucleus of heavier mass with the release of great amounts of energy, as in a hydrogen bomb.

The actual fireball produced by this appalling contrivance is some three miles in diameter (compared to 450 yards for a nominal bomb), and the crater, one mile across. Up to a distance of three or four miles from ground zero, total destruction could be expected; up to fifteen miles, severe damage from the blast; lighter damage would occur up to twenty miles. The blast effect at fifteen miles has been calculated as equivalent to a 1000 mph wind. Any of the largest cities in the world would thus suffer virtual annihilation from just one bomb.

The fire risk is equally terrifying. Persons exposed in the open four miles away would receive fatal burns; eight miles away very severe burns; and up to twenty miles away progressively slighter burns. Fires would occur as much as fifteen miles from ground zero. The heat "flash" from the bomb lasts from ten to thirty seconds—much longer than from a nominal bomb. So much of it could be escaped at moderate ranges by taking cover.

The immediate radiation or "gamma flash" is of no importance since its range is so much less than that of the other effects. The H-bomb may produce, however, two tons or more of fission products compared with the five-pound yield of the nominal bomb. Residual radiation therefore becomes of very great importance with this weapon, and will be discussed at some length in the next chapter.

Problems of Delayed Radiation

Problems of Delayed Radiation

The direct radiation from the radioactive cloud produced by an atomic explosion is effective for about a minute only—until the cloud has risen into the upper air. Radiations continue to be emitted from it, however, with decreasing intensity. Radioactive substances "decay" at varying rates, which average out for the fission products of the bomb thus:

For any given rate of radiation or dosage at a time one hour after the explosion, the rate after

7 hours	will be 1/10
2 days	will be 1/100
2 weeks	will be 1/1,000
3 months	will be 1/10,000

The fine particles of the cloud take a long time to settle back to earth. When eventually they do settle, the remaining radioactivity is negligible. There is, therefore, little obvious hazard from fallout due to an explosion taking place in the air. This applies to a nominal bomb which would probably be exploded at a height of about one thousand feet to obtain the maximum blast effect. Some localized neutron-induced surface radioactivity would occur but would be well decayed by the time rescue operations reached the area.

The H-bomb, by contrast, provides a very adequate blast for any conceivable purpose even if exploded at ground level. In this case, in addition to the fission products themselves, large quantities of earth and water are vaporized and rendered highly radioactive. The resulting particles settle much more quickly than the original bomb products. In a test at Bikini, using a 14-megaton bomb, an area over two hundred miles long and forty miles wide, in a downwind direction, was heavily contaminated. This is equal to a large part of southern England, whence the menace to a small country can be broadly appreciated.

Most of the fallout is deposited within one hundred miles of ground zero, but enough to be dangerous is carried to much greater distances. The total doses of radiation that would have been received by a person in the open in the first three hours after this incident, at various distances, have been estimated as follows:

At 5 miles from ground zero 5000r

At 105 miles from ground zero 2000r

At 160 miles from ground zero 500r

At 190 miles from ground zero 300r

and the fallout decays in the manner described above. Under substantial cover the dose rate for most of the affected area would be so reduced as to be safe as regards life at least. Basements or slit-trench shelters with a three-foot covering of earth afford the best protection, and within them only about 1/300 the above doses would have been received. For lack of these a ground-floor room as far as possible from outside walls is fairly effective.

The amounts of radiation which can be tolerated by a human being, during various periods of time, are still a subject of controversy. A single dose of 50r produces no observable effect and therefore might be regarded as a permissible dosage during one day, provided there was no further exposure for several weeks. Under emergency conditions, the following figures have been suggested as safety limits:

50r in 1 day,

25r daily for 3 or 4 days,

5r daily for 2 to 3 weeks.

A number of instruments exist for measuring dose rates in an area, or total dose received during a period of exposure. Civil defense personnel are equipped with these and would thus, by working in shifts, be able to carry out rescue and decontamination[1] operations with minimum danger.

The basic precaution against fallout from nuclear explosions is thus to remain under cover—the most solid cover possible—for forty-eight hours after an incident. With the aid of radiation-detection instruments, populations can then be advised when it has become definitely safe to emerge.

Anyone who for any reason has to be in the open when there is risk of contamination should use close-fitting clothing, including headgear, scarf, gloves and boots, to exclude dust as completely as possible. In addition, any possibility of inhaling radioactive dust must also be guarded against. Any antigas

---

1. **decontamination:** the action of making (an object or area) safe for unprotected personnel by removing, neutralizing, or destroying any harmful substance, as radio-active material or poisonous gas.

respirator or a simple smog mask is effective and in an emergency even a handkerchief tied round the face would do.

Decontamination

Objects contaminated by radioactive dust or water eventually become safe simply by natural decay of the radioactivity. The process cannot be accelerated or otherwise altered by any known chemical or physical means, but simple decontamination methods can be employed.

The basic principle is the liberal use of water. Large surfaces such as streets, walls, etc., can be dealt with by hosing down, as with fire-fighting equipment. The water used should be disposed of into drains where the removed radioactivity is harmless. Smaller objects should be well scrubbed, and the free use of detergents is recommended for them and for personal use. Contaminated clothes can be treated likewise, though if very heavily affected would be best disposed of altogether. Burying is the best method of disposal, and should be done as far as practicable from human environments. *Burning merely carries the radioactivity into the atmosphere, and is definitely to be avoided.* Any surface or substance with a porous or rough surface or which for any reason cannot be thoroughly cleaned should likewise be disposed of.

Food and water are unaffected by direct radiation (gamma rays), but might be poisoned by fallout. The dangers resulting from taking into the body even minute amounts of radioactive material are so great, in this connection, that no precautions can be too stringent. Where buildings are still standing and where food is covered up, there should be little risk. In the area of total destruction, however, food might well be rendered radioactive by neutrons and should be regarded as unsafe. Otherwise, solid foodstuffs, e.g., meat, cheese, butter, would normally be rendered usable by removing a quarter of an inch all around. More porous foods such as bread, biscuits, etc., would be best ditched. Tinned foods would be safe, but one should wash the outside of the tin well before opening.

Water supplies might be somewhat affected, but most of the fallout would sink to the bottom of a reservoir, and could be removed completely by the ordinary domestic water softener.

In any case of doubt, the final arbiter[2] of safety is the contamination meter issued to civil defense authorities, who should be called in at once in such an instance.

In the case of some observations on soil, some 80 percent of the deposited radioactivity was found to remain in the upper one-inch layer after a year's weathering. This suggests that dangerous substances could be taken up by plants, and thus by animals and humans, over a long period of time. Plants are much less sensitive than man or animals to radiation, and thus would not suffer a lot of damage themselves.

---

2. **arbiter:** literally, a person who has the sole or absolute power of judging or determining. Used figuratively in this sense.

Book One
Chapter Six

Long-Term
View

Long-Term View

The long-term effects in survivors of the bombing in Japan, as observed by an international group of physicians in 1955, give food for thought and will be detailed briefly here.

The most serious matter, in the opinion of the writer, is the persistence of vague ill health, tiredness, increased susceptibility to infections and other common disorders, and mental fear or apathy. By the word *persistence*, a term of years is meant. Evidence has been adduced[1] indicating that physical and mental retardation of growth occurred in children who survived the bombings. This, on the larger scale of global war, could only have the most serious consequences for the human race.

Leukemia and other blood disorders, most of them invariably fatal, were appearing in survivors at a considerably higher rate than in unexposed populations, though the peak year was 1950. Cataracts[2] were also relatively more common. These, incidentally, are thought to be due possibly to neutron irradiation in particular; further, their distribution has suggested that the range of neutrons may be much greater than is commonly accepted.

---

1. **adduced:** brought forward in argument or as evidence; cited as pertinent or conclusive.
2. **cataracts:** areas in the lens of the eye which have become opaque due to disease, causing partial or total blindness.

Many male survivors had become sterile as a result of exposure to radiation, and an additional rather alarming figure was the increase in major congenital[3] malformations among the children of those people who retained fertility. An increase by 72 percent on the rate common in unexposed populations was found. That is to say, there have been nearly twice as many abnormalities in the children of these survivors as one would find among an average group.

The above observations refer, of course, to people who received a single large dose. What of the effects of small repeated doses spread over many years?

Some investigations carried out in the United States on a number of radiologists revealed some interesting facts.

The average life span of this particular group of doctors was five years less than that of other doctors and of the general population (sixty years compared with sixty-five years).

The incidence of fatal leukemia was eight or nine times higher than that in nonradiologist doctors.

The average number of children born to members of the group was about half that found with other physicians (1.7 compared with 3.0).

Finally, there were 24 percent (one quarter) more congenital abnormalities among children of radiologists than among those of other doctors.

The group considered must have received, due to occupational hazard, perhaps as much as 1000r over a whole lifetime in

---

3. **congenital:** of or pertaining to a condition present at birth, whether inherited or caused by the environment, especially the uterine environment.

some cases, though in others probably very much less. This is a large amount compared with what an average individual receives. The figures nevertheless illustrate clearly the menace of chronic irradiation.

Every person during his or her life is continually bombarded with radiation in small quantities. Radioactive substances are everywhere present, though in minute amounts and cosmic rays from outer space contribute to the total background radiation.[4] This normally amounts to about 1.5r in every ten years, 9–10r during a whole lifetime. In addition, diagnostic X-ray procedures give a certain dose to the subject. The average total receipt from this source is very difficult to estimate, but may be, for the reproductive tissues (gonads[5]) specifically, about 3r in thirty years.

The effect of chronic irradiation seems to be similar to the process of aging, to the extent that each roentgen is thought to shorten life by about a ten-thousandth. This in an average human being would only amount to a total of a few weeks due to background dosage. The general debility[6] and increased liability to infections already referred to, while less dramatic, present a far more serious prospect in terms of world health and working capacity.

Genetic Effects

Nuclear radiation does not produce monstrosities in babies just like that. This all-too-common idea is mere superstition.

The reproductive tissues of all living organisms produce

---

4. **background radiation:** the low radiation from cosmic rays and trace amounts of radioactive substances naturally present in the atmosphere.
5. **gonads:** organs in which reproductive cells develop in the male or female; sex glands. Ovaries and testicles are *gonads*.
6. **debility:** weakness or feebleness, especially of the body.

naturally a certain number of "mutations"—that is, hereditary[7] patterns in sperm or egg cells which differ to a greater or lesser extent from the normal for that species. Most of these result in infertility of the cell concerned, and they therefore never actually appear in offspring. Nearly all the remainder produce deleterious[8] abnormalities. (Beneficial changes are rare.) All that irradiation does to the gonads in doses insufficient to kill the cells, is to increase the rate of production of mutations. A total amount of about 50r received by an individual during his or her reproductive lifetime would double the total number of mutations produced during this period. Most of the changes, while deleterious, are also recessive—in other words, they may not appear in one or several generations but will eventually.

However, to take a very possible example, it is suggested that a total dose of 10r (in addition to "background") to every person in the United States might well cause the actual appearance of 50,000 cases of inherited defect, over and above the present "normal" number (2 percent), in children of the first generation born thereafter. Continuing this rate of dosage to succeeding generations, the figure would increase, ultimately reaching a steady half million per generation. Such a situation would pose a considerable social problem. A dose of only 1r to every person in the United States could produce several thousand cases of definite, if not obvious, handicap in the first generation. These figures, if expanded to cover the whole population of this planet, evidence the danger to which mankind is now exposing itself.

The situation cannot obviously be assessed fully at the present time. There may be a considerable error, one way or the other, with estimated figures, but the danger must not be ignored merely on this account.

---

7. **hereditary:** passing, or capable of passing, naturally from parent to offspring through the genes.
8. **deleterious:** harmful, injurious.

How much is man-made radioactivity actually contributing at the present time to the total receipt of radiation by humans at large? Taking external radiation only, due to fallout, wastes from atomic plants, etc., the probable amount is less than half a roentgen in thirty years to any individual. If weapon testing were to continue at a higher rate, equal to the maximum re-corded so far for any one year, perhaps double this figure might be close to the truth.

This does not sound like very much and by itself is not. But taking into account increasing use of medical X-rays, and the very uncertain factor of internal radiation, the outlook is not quite optimistic. As already mentioned, a human being living in a Western country receives about 3r to the gonads from medical X-ray procedures, on the average. Some individuals, of course, receive much more. A routine abdominal X-ray involves a total dose of 1r per exposure, of which a proportion reaches the gonads. More prolonged investigations may deliver doses of 10–20r. Since every least amount of radiation received produces more mutations, there is good reason to be concerned that exposure from all sources should be kept down to the barest minimum.

Internal Radioactivity

The danger of actually taking into the body radioactive substances has been referred to. It is illustrated by the fact, observed before radioactivity was discovered, that of uranium miners at Joachimsthal, a mining town in Czechoslovakia, more than 50 percent died of cancer of the lung. This was later found to be due to the continuous inhalation of a radioactive gas and of radioactive dust.

Most of the products of an atomic explosion decay very rapidly, so that only the longer-lived ones can contaminate more remote parts of the world. No such dramatic effects as that in the miners are to be expected. The most important substance appears to be an element called strontium 90.[9]

Strontium 90 loses half its activity in twenty years, and being chemically similar to calcium, tends to accumulate in bone once absorbed. Furthermore, it is very difficult to remove once fixed in bone. Its presence can be a direct cause of cancer of the bone, and blood diseases, such as leukemia, can result from its action on bone marrow. In this situation, since the radiation source is so close to the living cells, the gamma- and beta-ray activity becomes important. Strontium 90 produces, in particular, beta and gamma rays.

It has been put forward that the quantity of strontium 90 in human bones at the present time is about 1/10,000 the "maximum permissible amount." This does not allow, however, for several important factors. First, the possibility of further atomic weapon tests or nuclear accidents; second, subsidence of radioactive dust from the upper atmosphere continues for some time after such an incident. The effect is therefore delayed. These two items may well reduce the apparent safety margin, in the figure given, by 10–20 times. Next, the rate of uptake[10] in children, particularly those younger than four years, is three times greater than the average. Children are also more sensitive to radiation than adults (a characteristic of growing tissues). Furthermore, the value for "the maximum permissible amount" taken in the above estimate is actually that permitted for persons occupationally in contact with radiation. The figure for the whole population should probably be at least ten times less.

---

9. **strontium 90:** a radioactive form of the element strontium (a pale yellow metallic chemical element), present in fallout from nuclear explosions. Strontium 90 can be absorbed into the bones in place of calcium, hindering further absorption of calcium and leading to weak bones.
10. **uptake:** absorption.

These considerations practically annul[11] the safety margin. Other radioactive substances, known as carbon 14[12] and iodine 131,[13] as well as unfissioned plutonium,[14] appear too in appreciable amounts. When all these are taken into account, the situation appears indeed serious.

11. **annul:** to reduce to nothing; obliterate.
12. **carbon 14:** a radioactive form of carbon which is used as a tracer in chemical and biochemical research. Also, because of its presence in all carbon-containing matter, *carbon 14* provides a means of dating archaeological specimens, fossils, etc., by measuring the amount of radioactive *carbon 14* remaining in them. *See also* **tracer** in the glossary.
13. **iodine 131:** a radioactive form of iodine, used especially in the diagnosis and treatment of thyroid function, in internal radiation therapy and as a tracer. *See also* **tracer** in the glossary.
14. **unfissioned plutonium:** small particles of plutonium which have not undergone fission in a nuclear reaction. *See also* **plutonium** and **fission** in the glossary.

Book One
Chapter Seven

Treatment of Radiation Disease

Book One
Chapter Seven

Treatment of Radiation Disease

There is no specific *medical* treatment known at this time for the effects of nuclear radiation.

This is stated to clarify the matter for the reader. Some attention to the subject is not without point, however, since general first-aid measures are of value. Atomic warfare would bring about, inevitably, severe dislocation of hospital and other medical services. At Hiroshima, for example, a large proportion of the doctors and nurses in the city were killed by the explosion. As a result, it might easily be several days before a casualty received proper medical attention. The main burden of handling casualties would, therefore, fall on ordinary men and women with little medical knowledge.

The intention here is to outline the basic principles of first-aid treatment of atomic casualties.

It will be recalled that there are three major effects of the bomb—burns, mechanical injuries and radiation sickness. Any of these may be met with singly in some cases, but most commonly the casualty who is in serious need of attention will be suffering in varying degree from all three. For instance, radiation sickness, uncomplicated, would probably only occur as a result of fallout at some distance from the explosion. Simple burns would be due mainly to fires after the explosion where the person had been more or less shielded from gamma flash. Mechanical injury could occur where a building had collapsed onto a shelter which afforded adequate protection from immediate blast and flash. This is to give some idea of the conditions that could be expected in particular situations. The interested reader will be able to work out other possibilities and combinations for himself.

It is important to remember that combinations of the various types of effects produce a greater likelihood of death occurring or of grave illness than might be expected from the perhaps mild nature of each particular effect. For example, in experimental rats it was found that the burn involving 30 percent of the body surface together with radiation to the amount of 250r, brought about 100 percent deaths. Now, 30 percent body-area burn is by itself roughly an LD_{50} burn. 250r alone is nonlethal. Thus, combinations of moderate injuries may be highly lethal. Experiments with rats do not, of course, apply exactly to human beings but the same principle applies and will, in fact, be reinforced by the emotional and mental shock which is presumably much greater in humans.

The purpose of all first aid is twofold: firstly, to preserve the life of the patient and maintain his general well-being as far as is possible; and secondly, to prevent further injury or damage and avoid complications.

The first-aid treatment of burns and mechanical injuries is fully covered in many excellent popular books. It is not intended here to repeat this material in detail but rather to discuss the handling of cases from the point of view of the particular problems encountered in atomic warfare. The reader is recommended to study more simple books on first aid and learn the principles of emergency dressings, splinting of bone fractures, prevention of bleeding and artificial respiration.

Nuclear radiation attacks the vital processes of the body in such a way as to bring about a state resembling severe shock.

The maintenance of the general condition of the patient is of paramount importance—of far greater importance than the tackling of minor localized injuries. This applies also in burn and injury cases but much more so when these are complicated by a sizable dose of radiation.

Obviously, if the patient is bleeding severely or has a perforated chest wound, this must be dealt with first to avoid immediate death. The state of "shock," so-called, is of two kinds: True clinical shock is a physical condition of collapse of circulation as a result of loss of blood or loss of fluid volume from the circulation; it is characterized by coldness, clamminess and rapid, weak pulse. Emotional shock is the second variety, occurring often by itself and often in combination with the first. It will be met with, as already mentioned, on a large scale in connection with atomic incidents and requires mental rather than physical ministrations,[1] as discussed in the final part of this book.

Complete rest for the patient is vital and should be fairly easy to provide even if living conditions after an incident are somewhat primitive. This and all the procedures to be described should be continued until the patient is seen by a doctor who will be able to advise on further measures and will also be able to determine when activity can be gradually resumed. Sedation is of value in most cases and the simple sedatives available in most households can be employed in moderation without harm. In severe cases, particularly where there is pain, morphine may be indicated, but will however probably be only available to a few. Aspirin is useful, but as far as possible, the soluble varieties only should be used, since they are less irritating to the gut. The patient should be moved as little as possible particularly if there are fractures which would be at best fixed only with makeshift splints. The patient should be kept warm.

---

1. **ministrations:** acts or instances of giving help or care; service, especially in religious matters.

An adequate diet is essential to maintain the general vitality of the patient. Malnutrition in Japan in 1945 contributed not a little to the severity of the symptoms experienced by victims at Hiroshima and Nagasaki. However, a certain type of diet is required. It should be semisolid and contain little irritant roughage: coarse bread, tough green vegetables and the less digestible parts of meat should be avoided. Too much protein is a stimulant to the body processes so the amount of this type of food should be not more than the basic daily requirement. A total of two to four ounces of protein foods (cheese, meat, eggs) should cover this adequately. Plenty of vitamins and minerals would be valuable and could be obtained from fruit, yeast products and vegetables in the form of juices or purées.

The subject of fluids warrants special attention. Loss of fluid above the normal may occur in several ways. The injured case may have lost an appreciable amount of blood, and it is worth noting that from half to one pint can be lost into the site of a bone fracture without any more evidence of it than moderate swelling. Radiation damage to the gut brings about vomiting and diarrhea, through which many pints a day can be lost. Finally, the urine output may be increased on account of disturbance of the glandular mechanism controlling the kidneys.

The first-aid worker will not be able to do much more than ensure a sufficient intake of fluid by mouth, which should be such as to maintain a urine output of at least a quart daily. In a case where the kidneys are disturbed, of course, this will not be a reliable guide and more fluid should be given.

Victims who have lost much blood from any cause may need transfusions of blood, plasma or plasma substitutes, and such cases should have the first attention of doctors or trained personnel.

The body's ability to produce the substances which afford natural protection against bacterial infection is depressed by nuclear radiation. Furthermore, the depression of the blood-forming tissues means a great reduction in the white cells of the blood which constitute the first line of defense against infection. Great care must therefore be taken with matters of hygiene. The surface of the body generally and, of course, wounds in particular, must be kept as far as possible absolutely clean and the use of mild disinfectants would not be out of place. In a debilitated individual the nose and mouth are especially subject to bacterial attack and should therefore be washed out frequently. Where breakdown or destruction of normal sanitary arrangements has occurred, some means should be devised for disposing of excreta in such a way that minimum contamination of persons and foodstuffs is permitted.

Of therapeutics,[2] general and specific, little can be said. Drugs would inevitably be scarce and the average person has not the training to use them safely. To discourage vomiting, a good vitamin intake could be maintained as described above and the antiseasickness drugs if available are fairly harmless and may help.

Such drugs and equipment as are available will have to be reserved primarily for intermediate-type cases where recovery is possible. Those who have received a small dose of radiation will normally clear up without treatment. The recipients of lethal or near-lethal doses are so likely to die that it will probably be uneconomical to expend much time or expensive treatment on them. The onus[3] of distinguishing between types of cases and allocating drugs will, of course, rest with qualified physicians; first-aid measures should be applied all round.

The prevention of radiation disease has been investigated.

---

2. **therapeutics:** the branch of medicine that deals with the treatment and cure of diseases; therapy.
3. **onus:** difficult obligation, task, burden, etc.

Certain substances were found effective if given immediately *before* exposure, but their protective action wore off so rapidly that they did not represent a practical method.

The removal of absorbed radioactive substances is a difficult matter; various dietary procedures have been tried, but few have met with consistent success.

However, research done by L. Ron Hubbard has indicated that a precise combination of vitamins in specific doses, when administered as part of a regimen designed to flush toxins out of the body, can be of value in handling the effects of radiation. Alleviation of some of the effects and increased tolerance to radiation have been the apparent result.

In all these rather depressing aspects of radiation, the factor of expense and/or scarcity of equipment looms large. The highly workable ideas of L. Ron Hubbard presented in this book are therefore doubly welcome.

Dr. F.R. Spink is a graduate of medicine and surgery from Cambridge University, England. He currently maintains a practice in the UK.

Man's Inhumanity To Man

by L. Ron Hubbard

Book Two
Chapter One

The Real Threat of Atomic Radiation

Atomic radiation does constitute a real threat in today's society.

You should realize that on the face of Earth today there is no ready solution for radiation. We are talking about an unsolved problem, one which could be solved with some brilliant work. Scientology is already doing its part in solving it.

Scientology philosophy is the study and handling of the spirit in relationship to itself, universes and other life. Scientology means *scio*, knowing in the fullest sense of the word and *logos*, study. In itself the word means literally *knowing how to know*. The technology of Scientology encompasses many aspects of life, and is expounded not as something to believe, but as something to *do*.

Nuclear fission is an interesting subject and deeply concerns the Scientologist. Why? Because Scientologists are interested in health and where there is a radioactive atmosphere there is also a declining health rate.

Tiredness, exhaustion, hopelessness and apathy all go hand

in hand. These are the Four Horsemen[1] of today. If I tell you that one of the most important parts of human thinkingness[2] is the ability to confront a future or to have a future or to find a future, and if I tell you at the same time that nuclear fission says to you "You will have no future," you can at once see that it has depressing mental aspects which have not been broadly presented to the world.

A man's future normally depends upon his own actions, his ability to get on with his fellow men, his ability to do work, to make himself personable, to maintain his home and raise his family. Not so long ago, in the southwestern part of the United States—which was, incidentally, saturated with radiation at that time—a medical doctor, an apparently sane man, after investigating the effects of radiation on health and the way it influenced the future, shot and killed his wife and five children and committed suicide. He left a note saying that there would be no future for this race.

This is fairly grim. Hardly anybody knows anything at this time about nuclear fission. Hardly anybody has any idea of what it is doing, and here is probably its greatest menace. It is something which hangs in the air, something which sneaks in upon you, touching you, and of which you aren't aware.

We have man living in a mysterious world. He is getting sick from types of illness which his medical doctors do not glibly[3] diagnose. The doctor says it is gastroenteritis,[4] but of an "unknown kind," since he has not seen it before, and the patient has the idea that it may be radiation that is making him ill.

---

1. **Four Horsemen:** Four Horsemen of the Apocalypse: four riders on white, red, black and pale horses, symbolizing the pestilence, war, famine and death which are prophesied in the Apocalypse, or book of Revelation, the last book of the New Testament in the Bible.
2. **thinkingness:** potential of considering; the combination of past observations to derive a future observation.
3. **glibly:** done in a smooth, offhand fashion.
4. **gastroenteritis:** an inflammation of the stomach and the intestines.

Because he does not know and because this cannot be proven easily and because some governments today have been somewhat less than straightforward on this subject, there is no easy way to know what is taking place.

In other words, a man raises his family. He has lots of children running around. They are going to go to school and he goes to work every day to get money to support his family. He wants his children to be healthy and one day they are sick. He cannot understand quite how or why, but one day he realizes that there is a high probability that his children will never grow to maturity. They are growing into a world which will not be there and he says, "What is the use then? Why should I raise this family?"

That is very depressing and fills one with grave concern. I would never join the ranks of those who attempt to drive people into hysteria simply for their own gratification or political ambitions. I would at least attempt to discover and let people know the truth—truth without hysteria or question marks.

The First Danger of Radiation

So let us take up the subject of radiation very brutally, bluntly and factually, stressing this message: *The first danger of radiation is not small invisible particles drifting through the air, but the hysteria occasioned by the propaganda,[5] the misunderstanding and the threat which accompanies it.*

Hysteria is a danger because this hysteria could, unless expertly handled, grow to such a peak that whole populaces could go entirely out of the control of their own governments.

There are two ways of going out of control. One is to get upset and throw bricks through the prime minister's window or

---

5. **propaganda:** information, ideas or rumors deliberately widely spread to help or harm a person, group, movement, institution, nation, etc.

at the White House. The other way is simply to lie down and quit the game of life.

Somebody comes along and says, "Here, here, the streets are dirty. Clean them," and the sweeper says, "Why? What's the use? There is no future."

Somebody says to the schoolteacher, "Teach these children," and the teacher replies, "Why teach them? They will never live." Somebody says, "The factory's wheels must turn," and the mechanics say, "We are tired."

That is an aspect which the great powers may or may not have thought over. But it is the first real danger in the H-bomb at this time and it is an important aspect in which we, as Scientologists, are interested.

My Own Background

One might well ask what I know about this subject. It is amusing that I should know anything about it, because my basic reason for working in the field of the mind and life— Scientology—was based upon the use to which this information was being put in the early 1930s.

I was a member of the first class in nuclear physics[6]—we called it atomic and molecular phenomena, of which nuclear physics is just a small part—which was taught at George Washington University. It was not at that time, and is not now, an open-and-shut subject. It permitted speculation. Atomic and molecular phenomena was simply no more and no less than, "What did electrons and nuclei do when one did something to

---

6. **nuclear physics:** that branch of physics (the science of relationships between matter and energy) which deals with atoms, their nuclear structure, and the behavior of nuclear particles.

them?" and that included not only the study of individual atoms, but also what happened to bread crumbs when one threw them about.

This whole subject was being grooved down—not by anybody's choice or selection—to a very forceful study of splitting the atom, and the splitting of the atom at that time was a fact. Everybody thinks the atomic bomb suddenly blew into our knowledge, full-armed, in 1945 when we bombed Japan. This is not true.

The atomic bomb technology was developed rather fully for decades before anybody put it to use. It required somebody to sit down and write a check. The technology was there, but the tremendous amount of money necessary to develop nuclear physics had not been given. It was a war which made that possible. The check was written for three billion dollars and a bomb got manufactured.

Nuclear physicists were, in the thirties, known as "Buck Rogers[7] boys"—from the comic strip character of science fiction. There was nothing a nuclear physicist could be used for. He had no background that could be used in industry. Rocketry was completely flat and left to the Germans and the Russians. Any field that he might have entered had no real use for him, so he either employed himself as a civil engineer running a survey or something of the sort, or he turned to some other field of endeavor.

So after I finished training, the Depression was on in full and the only use I could put this Buck Rogers information to was science fiction. Like so many later physicists I wrote science fiction for years, and that was the only remunerative use I made of this material.

---

7. **Buck Rogers:** the main character of a popular American comic strip, later made into motion pictures. The stories were science fiction, set in the twenty-fifth century.

But as far as nuclear physics is concerned, the only use I ever made of any of the material directly and intimately was to try to define the tiniest particle or wavelength[8] of energy in this universe.

I realized that I would probably find that small particle in the human mind. I did a calculation to see how memory is stored and developed a theory that was called "The Protein Molecule Theory of Memory Storage." I wrote this simply as a possibility and then demonstrated later on in this thesis that it was an impossibility. The idea was that there were two to the twenty-first power binary[9] digits of neurons in the brain; each one of these protein molecules, with a hundred holes in it, would act as a storage battery for human experience. I did the calculation and found that if you took all the perceptions and observations of a three-month period and stored them, even this vast number of neurons was not sufficient to hold it. I asked people if they could remember anything earlier than three months ago and since most of them could, I decided that memory was not stored in protein molecules.

This theory came back from Austria as "an Austrian development" and in fact with exactly the same computation which I made back in 1938. But they didn't say that it was unworkable. They said that this was the way in which human memory is stored.

The search for the smallest particle led me over to the psychology department of George Washington University, and I asked what proved to be very embarrassing questions—such as "How do people think?" which was never answered but incoherently explained in a most unscientific manner. I was in the field

---

8. **wavelength:** the distance from any point in a wave, as of light or sound, to the same point in the next wave of the series.

9. **binary:** designating or of a number system which uses a base of 2 rather than the base of 10 used in the customary number system. The binary system uses combinations of the digits 0 and 1 to express all other numbers.

of engineering and here one had, for instance, a person such as a specialist in chemical material: when one went over to him to ask a question, he answered it. With a shock I received the information that there was no functioning department devoted to the human mind which could scientifically answer questions about it. Hence my interest quickened.

They could tell me a lot about the reactions of rats when put in mazes, but not how rats thought. They said the subject was called psychology, from *psyche,* a Greek word meaning "soul," but in the same breath told me that they didn't believe in a soul because it couldn't be proven. Here was, for my information, a serious hole in man's culture.

They considered the mind as a brain which had actions and reactions of various kinds. But as nearly as I could understand it, it had to be a mathematical subject which should be developed by observation of people. As far as I could discover, none of these things were being done. Psychologists were not mathematicians and did not know how to develop a theory mathematically and extrapolate it in such a way as to get a prediction of what the condition was.

When I asked where this subject came from, they answered that it was born in 1879, in Leipzig, Germany, from the mind of a man named Wilhelm Wundt.[10] But they had no textbook written by him and nobody seriously contributed to this subject. I got a suspicion that somebody was kidding somebody and was pretending to know something about something about which nothing was known.

I was shocked to discover that there was no Anglo-American technology of the mind—only some German guesses. This, to

---

10. **Wilhelm Wundt:** (1832–1920) German physiologist and psychologist; the originator of the false doctrine that man is no more than an animal.

me, was a serious thing. We are given to believe that the field of the mind is very definitely covered, that a great deal is known about it. I had just been studying a subject, nuclear physics, which threatened to disturb the mental equilibrium[11] of the world in future years. "Someday somebody will want to know something about the mind," I said to myself, and so I went on about my work, continued my studies, and as I wrote and lived and fought through the Second World War, my attention stayed on this research project. The materials just kept mounting up.

It seemed to me that it became more and more necessary that man should know something more about the mind. In view of the fact that some of my friends in World War II went a bit off their heads, I found that there was some use for knowledge about the mind and thinkingness.

Man Is Not a Machine

I found through continuous observation that *basically man is not a machine, however much he loves machinery. Whatever man consists of, he is basically NOT EVIL. He is merely ignorant.*

With these findings came a considerable amount of technical information concerning man's reactions to various stimuli such as electricity, light, smell—various types of reactions which culminate now in his reaction to nuclear fission.

The Revolt of the American Nuclear Physicists

At the end of World War II, a friend of mine—Lieutenant Commander of the Coast Guard, Johnny Arwine—and I went to

---

11. **equilibrium:** mental or emotional balance; evenness of mind or temper; composure.

the California Institute of Technology to meet with a great many old-time atomic physicists who had been at the project that exploded the original bomb at Alamogordo. It was our intention to organize these people so that some sort of sensible control could be monitored across the bomb. Nobody had thought about it at that date, and Johnny Arwine and I were still in uniform. We had both been in the world of engineering, then in the world of the arts and then finally in the service. Neither of us had had a thing to do with atomic fission[12] in its development.

We got these atomic physicists together and addressed them. We spoke of using a propaganda weapon against anyone who would use atomic fission further against the human race and using any means we had to educate the people in the world concerning this.

The nuclear physicists were already so furious about the misuse of atomic power for destruction that Arwine and I could not control the meeting. We couldn't get across any thought that was even rationally workable. These men said one thing: "We wish to overthrow the government of the United States by force."

That is an astonishing chapter in the field of nuclear physics which only a few of us know about. There was a revolt, and later on offices opened in the United States to propagandize the public in a movement led by the late Albert Einstein.[13]

Arwine and I failed and withdrew our support from that meeting and did our best to calm them. We reported the findings to the Navy Department and the President. We said that we could not associate our names with this organization. But the

---

12. **atomic fission:** the splitting of the nucleus of an atom into nuclei of lighter atoms, accompanied by the release of energy. This is the principle of the atomic bomb.
13. **Albert Einstein:** (1879–1955) German physicist, US citizen from 1940; formulated the theory of the conversion of mass into energy, opening the way for the development of the atomic bomb.

atomic physicist did try and he is not going to do much more because Albert Einstein is dead.

The other day I read the list of atomic scientists who are now dead. It is practically the whole roster. They died of leukemia, of cancer—the very diseases radiation sickness breeds. They died to a marked degree of radiation—mostly, I suppose, mentally, because they had exerted a tremendous overt act[14] against the world and had been unable to repair it in any way.

That is clear fact and not propaganda. I am just stating that there was a background where nuclear physicists did attempt to revolt. The punishment taken against him was severe. The information given here is not even vaguely confidential and I am not in the possession of any confidential material.

From that time on it was what seemed to be a lost cause. We knew that the world was certainly in danger from the fury of atomic war, but I am afraid that none of us were clever enough to realize that continued testing would take place, since it seemed so stupid. None of us counted on the factor that the air of the Earth would be polluted with radiation. That was not part of our understanding.

So the new thing that happened was that a certain carelessness for public welfare caused the continued testing of the atomic bomb.

Now let us examine this "revolt." And let us see in it the truth of the threat of hysteria. *Even the men who made the bomb became so hysterical for a while that they could not even calmly organize.* They screamed disgracefully at their own government. The

14. **overt act:** an act by the person or individual leading to the injury, reduction or degradation of another, others or their persons, possessions or associations. It can be intentional or unintentional.

danger was never that great, certainly. Defenses were being built, no new war threatened. Yet these men went a bit mad. The group could not be controlled. They would not even listen to the necessity of calm public education. They merely wanted more hysteria. By the actions of these persons can be predicted a possibility of hysteria on a much wider scale. Propagandists[15] to the contrary, this must be prevented.

I do not believe that atomic fission will continue being tested to a point where everybody dies. But I do believe that it will continue being tested to a point where everybody could get so worried that a great deal of the ability would be gone out of society.

I am not talking against the United States. The United States was simply the first to develop this. Since that time the bomb has gotten into much more irresponsible hands in getting into Russian hands.

In the final analysis, man has done an unfortunate thing, and unless defenses can be found and the public educated, he may very well pay a dreadful price.

What Is Radiation?

Radiation is either a particle or wavelength; nobody can say for sure. One moment everybody says it is a wavelength and the next they say it is a particle. Let's define it as *a capability of influencing matter, and that that capability can be exerted across space.*

A bullet can influence matter, and the only different definition we would make in atomic radiation is that it does it more so. Shoot a man and he dies. Spray a man with radiation and he dies more slowly, but he dies.

---

15. **propagandists:** people involved in producing or spreading propaganda. *See also* **propaganda** in the glossary.

A man does very specific things in the process of dying from atomic radiation. He dies in a certain way.

The oddity is that if you throw a handful of bullets at somebody he doesn't get particularly upset, as the bullets are just being tossed at him. Supposing tomorrow you throw another handful at him, and repeat this for some days: He would simply say that somebody every day throws bullets at him. All those bullets never will add up to being shot with one bullet.

That is the single difference with atomic radiation. Today we throw a few rays at somebody and tomorrow we again throw a few rays at the same man and we continue for a while doing this, and all of a sudden he dies—as though he had been shot with a bullet. In other words, the effect of radiation is cumulative.

If one wants to know exactly what it does and how it does it, one would go listen to any nuclear physicist giving a technical lecture on the subject. There are all sorts of interesting data about it such as that if one took uranium and refined it one would get an intolerant element known as plutonium. If too much plutonium gets smashed together with too much plutonium it explodes, gamma rays spray about, other elements are influenced and so forth. Plutonium is an intolerant element. It is artificially manufactured and very intolerant of itself.

The way one makes an atomic bomb is quite interesting. One takes a piece of plutonium at, let's say, the end of a stick and another piece at the other end of the stick. One fixes it so that the back piece of plutonium will slide and hit the front piece of plutonium, and then simply throws the stick. When the front piece of plutonium hits the ground, the back piece hits the front piece and it explodes. And that is a bomb! When it explodes it releases a tremendous amount of gamma and many other items much too lengthy to catalog. Each one of these items, in some separate way, might have a deadliness of its own. The various materials that are used as containers of these bombs, such as cobalt 60,[16] have the capability of killing people practically at a breath, making the bomb a bit more deadly than it already was. All an atomic bomb is, is the method of getting plutonium to "intolerate" itself and explode.

What is important is that such bombs, when they explode, leave in the atmosphere a residue of gamma, strontium 90 and several other elements, which cause a widespread coverage of the countryside with a deadly substance. It floats in the air and unites with the dust particles which then settle on the ground or still drift along causing an air pollution, unlike TNT.

If somebody tells one not to worry about the atomic bomb since it is just a bigger kind of TNT bomb, this person is being very nonfactual, because atomic fission and TNT are not comparable. It is the blast, the burn, the fragments of TNT that do the injury. It is the radiation plus the blast, the burn, heat, particles and explosion that do the injury in the atomic bomb.

The atomic bomb is like TNT united with a poison gas which does not settle or dissipate. It is an entirely different thing to be bombed with TNT and poison gas than it is to be bombed with a TNT bomb.

Air Pollution

When we speak of this residue of the exploded bomb, we speak about radiation in the air, or air pollution. This residue stays in the air for a very long time before it comes down to earth, and the way these bombs have been tested in some cases

---

16. **cobalt 60:** a radioactive form of cobalt, a hard, lustrous steel gray metallic element.

was to explode them so high that the residue would not drift down to the surface for another ten years.

Political Factors

Whatever political purpose there may be in exploding a bomb, it is quite certain that the continuous testing of bombs is destructive. In some people's eyes it may have enough political connotation that they think it is necessary to go on testing bombs. These bombs must be released to keep people aware of the fact that they are in the possession of certain governments. Russia is trying to keep in the picture to show the people of Earth that she has atomic bombs. In other words, we have an arms race which is out in plain view and which is different from building a battleship and sending it around the world.

We explode a bomb to show we have one. Nobody is to be condemned for this providing it is at the same time thoroughly understood that it may widely endanger health if done too often.

It seems as though the Russian and American governments are actually of the opinion that not enough nuclear fission explosions have been done to date to damage the health of mankind. However, none of the releases which have been put out so far are convincing on this subject, and the public is not convinced. As a result we fall into two schools of thought—the government release and the public reaction.

The Public Reaction to Atomic Radiation

The public reaction is best expressed by men of the press and these have a tendency to fight back against the government releases. Governments say that although they don't know what the roentgen(r) count must be in order to be fatal, they nevertheless feel, by experiments which they have not made, that the amount of radiation in the atmosphere at this time will not kill, deform or derange more than six thousand babies in the coming year.

The press gets hold of this and quite righteously criticizes this statement. It asks, "Where is your data and what is it? How do you know? What do you mean about supposing that six thousand babies are not important? Suppose one of them was yours?"

The Question Mark

Out of this we get a tremendous question mark. *Whether radiation is floating across the world or not is not the point. There is a question mark floating across the world.* Is it or isn't it there? The question mark is radiation itself.

How Radiation Hurts a Human Body

How does radiation hurt a human body? Nobody can tell, exactly, but the following may be crudely stated. A sixteen-foot wall cannot stop a gamma ray but apparently a body can. We thus get down to our number-one medical question: How is it that gamma rays go through walls but don't seem to go through bodies? We can plainly see that a body is less dense than a wall.

We have to go into the field of the mind if we cannot find the answer in the field of anatomy.

Resistance

I can fortunately tell you what is happening when a body gets hurt by atomic radiation. It *resists* the rays! The wall doesn't resist the rays and the body does.

A gamma ray doesn't often settle in the body. It goes through. But its passage through the body creates a sensation of some kind, which, if too recurrent, is resisted on the part of the cells and the body. This resistance itself brings about the "stop" chaos that one observes in "no future."

The reaction of the mind to the bomb is that "we have no future anymore." The body says, "Stop the gamma. Stop, stop . . ." and as this is going on all the time when we are bombarded with radiation, the body finally says, "I am stopped." The body senses that there is an influence around it which it must stop because its survival is being endangered. It feels that it must *resist* the rays in one way or another, and the body gets hurt.

Oddly enough, cosmic rays and X-rays act the same way.

The Effects of Radiation

The slighter effects of radiation, very generally and rapidly, take on some of these aspects: hives,[17] skin irritation, flushes of one kind or another, gastroenteritis, sinusitis[18] and "colds," colitis,[19] exhausted achy feelings in the bones, glandular malfunction and so forth. We are here looking at effects one would normally experience from an overdose of radiation.

The serious reactions of atomic radiation all sum up to cancer—bone cancer, lung cancer, leukemia, skin cancer and so on.

Cancer merely says, "We cannot go on. Procreation in an orderly fashion is no longer possible on a cellular level." As the cells feel that they can no longer procreate in cooperation with the body, they simply procreate in a wild and abandoned

---

17. **hives:** a disease in which the skin itches and shows raised, white welts, caused by a sensitivity to certain foods or a reaction to heat, light, etc.
18. **sinusitis:** inflammation of one or more sinuses in the skull. (*Sinuses* are the cavities in the skull connecting with the nostrils).
19. **colitis:** inflammation of the large intestine.

manner in some other direction. In other words, the cells are driven into an independent action or reaction in the lines of growth.

This leads to an erosive, corrosive death of tissue. It is associated with "no future" as a mental reaction.

What Man Faces

That is what man faces—not much, merely obliteration. There are other less important, less dramatic things which lie between the slight effects and the serious effects of radiation.

If Earth became charged with radiation in a war, for instance, a man who was never tired might one day start feeling tired. We find that he might be holding a mental image picture of Trafalgar Square.[20] We ask him what happened at Trafalgar Square and he cannot think of anything. He wasn't run over by a taxi, nothing startled him. Nothing happened there to account for this picture being held in his mind and yet he is "stuck mentally" in Trafalgar Square. Why? He got a blast of radiation at that point. The wind blew around the corner and stuck him in that spot because the wind had radiation in it. His body sensed it. He resisted it. He "stuck his sense of time" in Trafalgar Square.

Whenever one gets one of these overwhelming mysteries one gets mentally upset. How would such a man react? He would one day get tired of being tired. He would feel that he was going to die anyway and so he might as well do something desperate. He is being told to do something. He feels that he should react and he doesn't know in which direction he should react. That is the main problem. He cannot account for this effect

---

20. **Trafalgar Square:** one of the main public squares in London, named after the battle of Trafalgar, in which Lord Horatio Nelson's British fleet overwhelmingly defeated a large fleet of French and Spanish ships. Trafalgar Square has in it a 168-foot-tall monument to Lord Nelson.

upon himself but he thinks that there *must* be some accounting for it, so he assigns a cause to some other agency than radiation.

The Misassignment of Causes for Sickness

One will sooner or later find this man saying, "What is making us ill here in London is *cats!*" He thinks that if he kills all the cats everybody will be in good condition again. There is no actual reason for this sudden enthusiasm for killing all the cats in London, but somewhere he got the idea that they carry some disease or other.

Possibly somebody else will say that the government is the cause. They will want to kill off the government. This would be misassignment of cause. Someone might say that truck exhaust fumes are the cause for all the illness in the world. Then one would have people lying down in the streets preventing buses and trucks from moving in cities. These people would be looking for a cause for their ill health, and if they could not find one, they would assign it rather ridiculously.

Every time one gets some kind of national question mark of this character, misassignment of cause takes place and people start doing strange things. A country might not be in a war at all but her populace would possibly feel they were fighting.

For example, a man was on a tug in Pearl Harbor when Japanese were flying over and bombing the harbor. He told his men to pick up potatoes and throw them at the planes. The sailors stood there throwing potatoes at planes three or four hundred feet above them.

These men knew what was wrong. They knew it was the bombers and the bombs. If they couldn't do anything at all, they would have turned around and said that it was the captain's fault. Having no outlet for their expression of outrage and not being able to define the cause, they would fictitiously[21] assign it to something else.

Because men cannot do anything to strike back against this thing called radiation, they are then liable to strike at things which are not connected with it. One might thus eventually have a tumultuous,[22] hard-to-control society. *That is one of the real dangers of radiation.*

The Problem of Hysteria

The problem we face today is not the control of governments who are failing to control testing in radiation but actually the problem of continuing to control a populace which may get too tired to go on living or may revolt into a hysteria which defies control. *They are afraid of the next war—they cannot face it.*

One can see that right now in the newspapers. People are upset about radiation. We may say that if we influence the governments to stop testing and issue sensible information on the subject of radiation to inform the people what it is really all about, that would be a sensible course.

We have, though, a secondary course which is quite well open, and that pertains to the control of civil populace problems. How does one keep people fairly calm, cool and collected, braced up to it, in the face of this much danger and trouble? Because if one can keep them in such a mental state by showing them that they aren't going to be killed, by giving them some hope of one kind or another, they will come through where they otherwise would not.

---

21. **fictitiously:** of, pertaining to, or consisting of fiction; imaginatively produced or set forth; created by the imagination.
22. **tumultuous:** full of tumult or riotousness; marked by disturbance and uproar.

I state again that *the danger in the world today in my opinion, is not just the atomic radiation which may or may not be floating through the atmosphere, but also the hysteria occasioned by that question.*

Book Two
Chapter Two

Radiation in War

Radiation in War

The use of atomic radiation as a weapon in war has been controversial for some time. Movements have been initiated suggesting that all future fissionable materials should be exclusively used for peaceful purposes. There has been a great deal of pressure on the governments of the world to stop bomb tests and not to pollute the atmosphere.

Even the governments themselves make such statements to the press—Russia says that we should be very peaceful about this, and the United States makes similar statements and the other nations all urge the cessation of atomic bomb testing.

I am sure that the president of the United States would abolish atomic bomb manufacture and testing if at any time he could feel with conscience that he is protecting the United States. However, he feels that he must protect his country and feels that the atomic bomb is a weapon which is capable of doing that.

Governments like the United States, Britain and Russia are pressured consistently much closer to home than some church organizations or public groups.

The German Nuclear Physicists' Revolt

In the last chapter I told you about the American nuclear physicists' revolt which failed in the United States in 1945. A similar revolt occurred in Germany in 1957. This was reported in a newspaper article which read: "Scientists won't make H-bombs. Eighteen top German scientists led by seventy-eight-year-old Otto Hahn, a pioneer of nuclear fission, today told Chancellor Adenauer,[1] 'We refuse to take any part whatsoever in making, testing or firing atomic weapons.' "

The revolt which failed in the United States continued in other countries. It is very difficult to find a nuclear physicist today who will stand in and read the meters, who will do the mathematical computations or anything else. These men are men too. They have families and they know very well that their own children, their wives and themselves could be made very ill and that civilization, which they have been brought up to cherish, is likely to disappear in the next war. That is as undesirable to them as it is to us or any other citizen anywhere else in the world.

What is a government up against? Why doesn't a government simply say, "Well, this is an undesirable weapon, and we will dispense with it"?

The Use of Science in War

Modern governments have gone very deeply into the world of science in order to execute their battles. At one time governments depended exclusively upon a man with a weapon in his hand. They depended on him to go in and bring about a better state of compliance on the part of some neighbor. They no longer depend on that soldier. They have developed weapons that are much more important to them than the courage of infantry.[2] These weapons have also already been used in World War II, so we are not talking about fictitious weapons. Every bit of scientific

---

1. **Adenauer:** Konrad Adenauer (1876–1967), German statesman; chancellor of the Federal Republic of Germany (West Germany) (1949–63).
2. **infantry:** soldiers or military units that fight on foot, in modern times typically with rifles, machine guns, grenades, etc., as weapons.

lore which has been accumulated by scientists in the hope that it may better the lot of their fellow men has eventually been employed in the destruction of men.

This is a rather hideous commentary on the practices of man and begins long before we ordinarily think of its having begun. In 1870 Benjamin Hotchkiss desired to end war by developing a weapon so violent that no one would dare fight war, and he invented the Hotchkiss hand-operated machine gun. Machine guns have been used in war ever since.

One hears of the Nobel Peace Prizes. Alfred Nobel discovered dynamite. TNT and dynamite were invented to make war so horrible that man would not fight it. We see a reflection of that aim in the Nobel Peace Prizes. Nevertheless, Nobel invented something that laid European cities and London in ruins in World War II. He wanted no more war, so through threat and fear and duress he thought to drive men into an opinion that war could no longer be fought.

This has always been the case. One hired a big enough army, armed it well, taught the enemy that it was sufficiently ferocious and thought that war would be too horrible for an enemy to fight. But every time it has brought war. Evidently war is not a good method of controlling other nations since it has never worked. Man should observe from the errors of the past that this method never will work.

Scientific Weapons

Today man is using scientific weapons. The scientific complexities which lie back of airplanes, bombs and so forth are quite fantastic. Some of them, such as proximity bombs, have two thousand separate connections per weapon. The most intricate thing one ever saw is one of these radar-shell antiaircraft[3]

---

3. **antiaircraft:** designed for or used in defense against enemy aircraft.

weapons. And they are quite deadly. They throw ammunition up into the vicinity of an aircraft and as it explodes it is made certain by the antiaircraft radar that the plane is in its center. These are called proximity shells. It was those shells which made it possible for US battleships to sail close to the very shores of Japan during the end days of World War II.

Brainwashing—a Political Weapon

How much further has man gone?

In 1927 or 1928 he developed a political weapon called "brainwashing." A Russian by the name of Ivan Petrovich Pavlov,[4] who had been experimenting with the reactions and conditioning of dogs, was brought to the Kremlin[5] by Stalin.[6] He was put in a separate room and was asked to write everything he knew concerning the conditioning and actions of animals as it might apply to the human being. He wrote a four-hundred-page manuscript which since that day has never left the Kremlin.

Immediately after that, in 1928, we saw the astonishing factor of cabinet ministers and Russian officials confessing to the most outrageous crimes. These men walked up before the bar of justice and at their own trials condemned themselves glibly. That was the first the world saw of brainwashing. In the Korean War, less expert people used these same techniques on the troops who were employed by the United Nations.[7]

---

4. **Ivan Petrovich Pavlov:** (1849–1936) Russian physiologist; noted for behavioral experiments on dogs.
5. **Kremlin:** the chief office of the government of the Soviet Union, in Moscow.
6. **Stalin:** Joseph Stalin (1879–1953), Russian political leader. As general secretary of the Communist Party, he expelled those who opposed him and ordered the arrest and deportation to Siberia and northern Russia of tens of thousands of members of the opposition. He became premier of the Soviet Union in 1941, and established himself as virtual dictator.
7. **United Nations:** an international organization with headquarters in New York City, formed to promote international peace, security, and cooperation under the terms of the charter signed by fifty-one founding countries in San Francisco in 1945.

Brainwashing is child's play. One shouldn't be very worried about it. Some 20 percent of the soldiers who are captured in battle will crack up in prison camps, and brainwashing does not violate this percentage. The man who invented it and the people who have used it are not sufficiently acquainted with the mind in order to make it very effective. An inspection of brainwashing cases demonstrates that it worked only occasionally.

What Brainwashing Is

Brainwashing is a very simple mechanism. One gets a person to agree that something *might be* a certain way and then drives him, by introverting him and through self-criticism, to the possibility that it is that way. Only then does a man believe that the erroneous fact is a truth. By a gradient scale of hammering, pounding and torture, brainwashers are able to make people believe that these people saw and did things which they never did. But its effectiveness is minor, as Russia does not know enough about the human mind.

Nevertheless, Pavlov himself, directing the use of his original manuscript, was certainly effective on the top Russian officials in those treason trials that shocked the world in 1928. These men never did anything that they admitted to having done. They simply had been conditioned into believing they had.

Brainwashing was attempted on Cardinal Mindszenty[8] in Hungary in 1948. It didn't work, but for a moment he quivered and wavered at his trial. Brainwashing is not an effective weapon, but it could be worked on, developed, and with the information about the mind denied to the rest of the human race and kept secret, brainwashing could be made to be effective.

8. **Mindszenty:** Jozsef Mindszenty (1892–1975), Hungarian primate (highest ranking bishop in the country) and Roman Catholic cardinal. An opponent of communism, he was arrested by the Hungarian government in 1948.

If that happened society could be made into slaves.

Knowledge about the Mind Must Not Be Kept Secret

Anything which is known about the mind and has benefited human beings must be permitted to exist in public view. It must be possible for anyone to lay his hands on how to undo such things as brainwashing. Therefore there must never be a restriction of technologies concerning the human mind. These must never be buried. There must never be a hierarchy in some universities that dictates the only technique that may be used or which invalidates the abilities of people who can work in the field of the mind.

It would be a very dangerous thing to the human race if such a group existed. Why? Because we have this thing called brainwashing and because it became a war weapon.

How to Undo Brainwashing

How does one undo brainwashing? One simply brings the person up to present time.[9] He is stuck in time—the time he was "brainwashed." He is thrust into the past. He is completely introverted, and all one has to do is to extrovert him, let him see where he is, how he is and what he is doing, and brainwashing desensitizes.[10] It is not even a problem to a trained Scientologist— we have undone with success many cases who have been brainwashed—but it is a problem to the governments of the world.

Governments fear that if we go into the next war and the enemy captures many of our troops, throws them into prison

---

9. **present time:** the time which is now and which becomes the past almost as rapidly as it is observed. It is a term loosely applied to the environment existing in now.
10. **desensitizes:** becomes less sensitive; becomes less affected or likely to be affected by a specified stimulus.

camps and brainwashes them, they will then so derange, disarrange and change these soldiers' loyalties that these men will return to their own country as saboteurs[11] and provocateurs.[12] It worries governments as this is a dreadful thing, for they depend on loyalty. And the fact that it might be possible to change the loyalties of individuals worries governments.

Any trained Scientologist with an E-Meter[13] could tell if somebody's loyalty had been changed. That is not even a problem, but it is a problem of governments and they are working in their own way trying to solve that problem. However, they don't seem to be making much progress.

The government itself is threatened by the weapon called brainwashing. Here is the head of state. He appoints some secret police and they play false and grab hold of the head of state and brainwash him. How can one assure his cabinet ministers that as he sits there at the head of the table he is not dictating the policy of some foreign nation? Such a condition could exist. It could happen.

Here is a weapon which is no good. It has not proven very useful. It is simply dangerous and it worries people. But it is a modern scientific weapon and its future history can only be dismal, because the only thing it can do is to shake the foundations of the governments which employ it. Russia must have various organizations posting guards every night around its leaders to make sure that nobody slips in and brainwashes them. How can one guarantee their loyalty to Russia?

---

11. **saboteurs:** people who engage in deliberate obstruction of or damage to any cause, movement, activity, effort, etc.
12. **provocateurs:** people who provoke trouble, cause dissension or the like; agitators.
13. **E-Meter:** an electronic device for measuring the mental state or change of state of *Homo sapiens.* It is *not* a lie detector. It does not diagnose or cure anything. It is used by auditors to assist people in locating areas of spiritual distress or travail.

If one suspects that one of one's associates has been brain-washed, the best thing to do is to get hold of a Scientologist for he can handle the matter with ease. But the real trouble is that few people have the skill to detect the fact of brainwashing and fewer still have the ability or technology to undo it. Because of this it becomes a terrible weapon.

It takes a very unsettled, unstable, neurotic personality to succumb to brainwashing. He has to be mad already, because Pavlov never did find out how to drive a really sane man insane. He merely found out how to utilize incipient madness.

The Problems of the Governments

I am only presenting this data about brainwashing to show that governments do have problems. You could say that radiation is not this kind of problem. A government uses radiation against the populations of other countries or against its own, therefore radiation could not be this kind of problem.

It is. Radiation is much more a deadly threat to a centralized government than it ever was to a population. That is an adventurous statement to make, but Russia will rue the day that she dabbled in brainwashing and she is certainly going to live to rue the day that she dabbled in atomic fission as a war weapon. How is this?

The History of War

One has to understand something about the history of war. Big tomes have been written on this subject, but I will briefly mention something about it.

The history of war is the history of *control*. The end goal of war is to throw out of its control the population of another government. This is just a little more advanced than the last definition of war in about 1792, which was rather lengthier and is summed up as follows: "to compel some compliance and obedience on the part of the other government." That is not really what war is supposed to do. War is supposed to throw another nation's population out of control so that one can supplant the government or its attitudes and give them their population back in control again.

War Against the Populations

Modern warfare is levied against the populations of other governments, on the theory that they will fall away from the controlling government and the controlling government will collapse and can then be changed.

Alexander the Great[14] did this much more rapidly. Whenever he went up against an enemy ruler he took his companion cavalry, rode through the ranks, found the enemy ruler and cut him to pieces. This was his idea of tactics and strategy. He has been criticized as a strategist because he didn't meddle with populations. He simply went and annihilated the other government. He wasn't really against the government or the household of the ruler. He didn't worry much about the population. He merely took it over.

He was very direct. He took the person out of control of the government by killing him. Modern war philosophy is different. It is to hammer and pound the population one way or another until it can no longer be controlled. The idea is that the government will then collapse. This is the basis on which modern war is fought.

Antipopulation Weapons

So now we use weapons which are antipopulation weapons. In World War I they didn't use a short sword at the throat of

---

14. **Alexander the Great:** Alexander III (356–323 B.C.), king of Macedonia, an ancient kingdom located in what is now Greece and Yugoslavia. By conquest, he extended an empire which reached from Greece to India.

Kaiser Bill.[15] They used machine guns aimed at the troops of Kaiser Bill. They overran the towns and villages and population. More modernly, they bomb the factories and cities so as to make the population give up. The population can no longer continue, therefore the government can no longer continue. In other words, the population is out of control.

The "Ideal" Weapon

What would be an ideal weapon to bring about this state? I am afraid it is a very sinful answer—namely, tested radiation. If one kept testing radiation, other populaces would get nervous. They would say "Can't we have peace one way or another?" In the face of radiation-impregnated[16] atmosphere one has a different attitude here, and a government which does not have radiation is apt to get worried about the governments who do, because an effect is being rendered against their population which they themselves cannot halt. Remember that there is no defense against a radiation-impregnated atmosphere at this time.

So one actually has the end goal of war being executed in times of peace simply by saber-rattling.[17] But this, again, is a very old philosophy. One took a large armed force and paraded it and everybody said, "We don't want anything to do with that army. Let's have peace with those people." They couldn't get any enthusiasm of the populace towards fighting. However, radiation is more sweeping, since it is not localized against the other government. So we have encountered an unlimited weapon without direction, since atomic testing is as deadly against one's own population as it is against the population of another nation.

---

15. **Kaiser Bill:** William II (1859–1941), emperor of Germany (1888–1918). (*Kaiser* is German for "emperor.") Through inept handling of his power and authority as emperor, he helped cause the circumstances leading to World War I and thereby the deaths of millions of men on the battlefields.

16. **impregnated:** infused or permeated throughout, as with a substance; saturated.

17. **saber-rattling:** a show or threat of military power, especially as used by a nation to impose its policies on other countries.

Here we get political problem number one of the atomic bomb. It can throw the very government that uses it out of control. It throws everybody out of control. The more it is tested or used, the more out of control populations get—for what is hysteria but the phenomenon of being out of control.

Unlimited Weapons

It is a historical fact that the history of weapons has brought up several which were unlimited and against which there was no known defense at that particular period. A weapon against which there is no defense becomes an unlimited weapon, and when these have appeared on the stage of man, governments have collapsed. Formal government cannot exist in the presence of an unlimited weapon.

This is a very factual, down-to-earth statement and it is something which appears in the textbooks of strategy and tactics. When one has a weapon against which there is no defense, governments become extinct.

The First Unlimited Weapon

There is a period which is covered mostly by legend between 1500 and 1200 B.C., where an unlimited weapon swept out of the steppes[18] of Russia and smashed any civilization which existed in Europe. It destroyed it so thoroughly that we haven't any records of it having happened, except in the poems of Homer.[19] Such early periods were considered very legendary until a German found the ruins of the city of Troy,[20] and it was

---

18. **steppes:** vast, treeless plains.
19. **Homer:** semilegendary Greek poet of circa eighth century B.C.: the *Iliad* and the *Odyssey* are both attributed to him.
20. **Troy:** ancient ruined city in Asia Minor, site of the Trojan War—a ten-year war waged against Troy by the Greeks to recover a Greek king's wife, Helen, who had been abducted by Paris, a Trojan.

concluded that Homer was writing about a real fight. However, according to Homer, this occurred before the history of Troy.

The horse and sword was the unlimited weapon which swept out from the steppes of Russia across Europe, just as it did in 1200 A.D. The nations of Europe were without defense against cavalrymen.[21] Infantry could not stand to a cavalryman. He was mounted, swift, his saber and sword penetrated any existing armor, and with or without formation or plan he could overrun any city. Nothing known then could stop him. It was not until Napoleonic times that men put pikes in alternate files and so stopped cavalry from charging and wiping up the infantry. But nothing like this stood against the cavalrymen as they came in from Russia.

These men carried everything before them. There was nothing like an organized government throughout the length and breadth of the Mediterranean or Europe for two hundred years.

Then somebody got a defense for it. Once more governments could exist, because a defense existed against the man mounted on a horse with his sword. That invention was the wall. That seems like an elementary invention but it certainly stopped this inrush of cavalry. Men could build a wall around their cities, could enclose their populaces and protect them against these expeditions which had rendered everything chaotic throughout Europe.

Not even the government on the steppes that originally sent those men survived their use. That government too was swallowed up and no record of its existence is left.

Where there is an unlimited weapon there is no government possible. Why? Because no city can be possible. Nobody can sit

21. **cavalrymen:** soldiers in the part of a military force composed of troops that serve on horseback.

down anywhere and govern from anywhere. The moment one actually sat down and started governing and communication lines started coming in and taxes were being collected, some irresponsible guerrilla band, no longer part of the enemy's regular army, would sweep down and destroy the city. No police were possible. There was no policing of the roads. Not even a man on a horse with a sword could fight a man on a horse with a sword. These tactics were not developed until centuries afterwards.

The only point which I am making is this: an unlimited weapon kills a government. A weapon against which there is no defense makes government impossible. That is why people today are worried about the atom bomb and why they would like to get together and sign a treaty which says "No more atom bombs, please."

What Is a Sovereign[22] State?

In international law we find that a *sovereign state protects the land and people of a country and a government is sovereign so long as it can* (and this is the crux of sovereignty) *protect the country and its people from aggressors.* When a government can no longer do so it senses the loss of some of its sovereignty.

A government is the government so long as it protects the land and citizens against an aggressor.

Now, what does an atomic bomb do to that? There is no defense against it. These weapons are going to come in as guided missiles at thousands of miles an hour. Only a few percent would have to get through to render everything in chaos, but more importantly, there is the saturation of the atmosphere

---

22. **sovereign:** having supreme and independent power or authority in government, as possessed or claimed by a state or community.

by radiation. That itself is unstabilizing the population, as it shows them it is impossible for a government to protect the population.

In the presence of an unlimited weapon a government tends to decentralize and disperse. It tends to leave the area of government and to govern from all over the place. That dispersal is already in effect in almost every nation on Earth. They are no longer governing from one place, but are spreading out into other cities. We are told it is because of the housing problem, but has one ever seen a government that wouldn't simply kick out a few tenants and make more room next door?

We look into this very carefully and find that governments have always been upset about unlimited weapons. They don't know what to do about them and therefore they are a much bigger problem to the government than to a populace, because government itself is trying to survive as itself, as a sovereign power.

If a government doesn't do something early in the career of an unlimited weapon, it no longer has the power to do anything about this. Sooner or later it has to realize that it is out of control. It will have to get into agreement with some other governments and do something about it. Their effort is continually to get some sort of treaty or agreement by which this thing won't be used.

It will have to be a very good treaty or agreement because man so far has always used—has never failed to use—the weapons he possessed.

The Value of Weapons

As far as any weapon is concerned, its total value is to upset the control capabilities of a government and its people. All a weapon is for is to unsettle this other government and throw it out of control.

But what about a weapon that throws one's own government out of control as well? Then it ceases to be a weapon. That becomes international suicide. Governments do not articulate this but they sense it and they endeavor to act in the direction of trying to do something before it is too late. Therefore there is no real need to pressure the government.

We Must Help the Government

People shouldn't go around pressuring the government and saying to the government that it has to abandon this or that, or mustn't do this or that. There is no sense really in throwing a vast number of rotten tomatoes at somebody on a governmental level simply because he hasn't come up with a solution. The poor man probably has been sitting up all night thinking about how the government has to be kept going with such a crisis hanging over his head.

What the government needs is solutions, assistance and help. But what reaction do we get against the government? We get "We won't work in this field anymore." "We are not going to help you." Pure hysteria.

There are people who will help governments. But the governments are so used to nobody helping them that after a while they tend to despair. It would be up to anybody who knew something about the subject to give them a hand because their power is already crumbling on the subject of atomic radiation. They need to be bolstered up.

Governments of the Western world know or sense these problems. They would give anything for some good solutions.

All the government needs to know how to do is defend against an atomic bomb or get a good enough reason to abandon atomic bombs.

The Atomic Bomb Is Not a Weapon

Let's be less vague about this. One cannot successfully use radiation in war. To call it a war weapon or to call it a weapon at all is being foolish. It is not a weapon, for a *weapon that kills off everyone or makes future control impossible by anyone everywhere and which kills off one's own people as well is not a good war weapon*. It is not useful in war.

If the United States were to bomb Russia, the amount of radiation thrown into the atmosphere would be so great that the population of the United States would probably be wiped out by the effect of its own bombs, without Russia having retaliated. There would be a tremendous amount of atomic fission generated in the atmosphere of Russia. There would be enough radiation in the air to seriously affect the population of the United States.

Similarly, if Russia bombed the United States, there would be enough radiation in the atmosphere—atomic testing for twenty years wouldn't accumulate the amount of radiation set off—that the residue would come back over to Russia which is but a very short distance away over the North Pole. The next thing would be that the Russian population would be in very poor condition.

International Suicide

So what is this thing? As it is not a practical war weapon one must then consider it a sort of bogyman. Everybody's hoping that nobody will find this out about it. But it might be used in war. Nations *do* commit suicide. Japan committed suicide in World War II, although one may not have noticed it. She knew very well that she might not win against the United States and England combined. Japan's own officers were known to make this remark. But they had to "save face," and rather than have their honor go completely overboard, they were perfectly willing to commit suicide by attacking the United States. That they were committing suicide is rather evident because they did not follow up their attacks seriously. Maybe if they hadn't been committing suicide they might have accomplished more than they did.

Russia, at its national mental level, has been known to do suicidal things, and to say that the fact that it kills everybody will prevent somebody from using the bomb is folly.

If it is a weapon, against whom is it one? Nobody knows. It really is a calamity. "It is too bad they ever thought it up"—a line which I caught from a New York taxi driver. He said, "It's too bad they ever thought that thing up." That was his total comment on it.

A later comment from a London taxi driver: "Isn't it a shame they thought it up?" Neither man had met the other, but they were both certainly in agreement that it is not a weapon but a regrettableness.

The use of the bomb could be international suicide.

All the governments of the world are practically fixated on the idea of atomic fission, which is no weapon and puts them, as we say in Scientology, in a no-game condition.[23] Almost any upstart little nation could suddenly come forward and develop something which *was* a weapon against which we had no immediate defense—but against which there was a defense—and immediately enforce its will upon the world. Another, better weapon than the H-bomb could enter the world and win!

---

23. **no-game condition:** a condition in which no game is possible, defining *game* as a contest of person against person or team against team. A game consists of freedoms, barriers and purposes. There is *freedom among* barriers. If the barriers are known and the freedoms are known, there can be a game. A no-game condition would therefore be a totality of barriers or a totality of freedom.

Has there ever been a simple weapon, managed by a few, that conquered large areas of Earth? There was.

The Assassins[24]

The government of Arabia in 1200 A.D. knew very well what a weapon was. It was a trooper. With his sword and shield and bow, his formations and officers, this man drawn up in ranks was a weapon. The cavalry had worked up to a tremendous peak, which one hears about in the incursions[25] of Genghis Khan.[26] All the governments in the Middle East knew the value of this weapon.

But there was a man by the name of al-Hasan ibn-al-Sabbah, and he had an offshoot Muslim cult of Ismailian Shiites[27] known as the Assassins. Al-Hasan operated from a mountain fortress which was so strong that it defied conquest for hundreds of years.

In the middle of its courtyards, al-Hasan created a heaven of milk and honey—with actual rivers of milk. He hired a number of houris[28]—lovely girls—and taught them how to amuse a man. He then sent some of his men with hashish[29] to spot a good-looking, rather stupid young man. They gave him some hashish

---

24. **Assassins:** a secret terrorist sect of Muslims of the 11th to 13th century who killed their political enemies as a religious duty. The word "assassin" comes from the Arabic name for this group, "Hashshashin," meaning "addicts of the drug hashish," as hashish was used by the leaders of the group to incite members to assassinate intended victims.
25. **incursions:** hostile entrances into or invasions of a place or territory, especially sudden ones; raids.
26. **Genghis Khan:** (1162–1227) Mongol conqueror of most of Asia and of East Europe. He was known to be ruthless in war, but he built an empire which lasted until 1368.
27. **Ismailian Shiites:** a fanatical sect of Muslims who are in disagreement with many of the accepted doctrines of the main group of Muslim believers.
28. **houris:** beautiful virgins provided in Paradise for all faithful Muslims.
29. **hashish:** a drug made from the resin contained in the flowering tops of hemp, chewed or smoked for its intoxicating and euphoric effects.

at the local inn, knocked him out and put him in a basket on a donkey and took him back to the stronghold. When he regained consciousness he was sitting in Paradise, with forty black-eyed houris and rivers of milk and honey.

When he asked, "Where am I?" he was told quite glibly and promptly, "Son, this is heaven. You've arrived." They let him stay around for two or three days. He found this very pleasant and wanted to stay for a long time, but they said, "You have been brought to heaven prematurely. It is necessary that you perform a small task for Allah, and if you are sure to get yourself killed in the performance of this task, and if it is successful, we can guarantee that you will appear again in heaven."

They slipped him some more hashish and took him down the mountain. He was placed in the vicinity of a palace. Now he had been told that the one deed that would get him back into heaven would be the assassination of the sultan who lived in that palace. The sultan out for his morning ride, surrounded by guards—who were the weapon of the day—would behold a young man, scimitar[30] in hand, leaping out of the crowd, and off would go the sultan's head. Of course, the guards would punch this young man full of holes and he would be dead.

Then the Old Man of the Mountain[31] would inform the people that the Assassins were the authors of the deed, and all that group had to do or infer was that some ruler at whatever distant realm or clime had done something displeasing to the Assassins and that they now required three camel loads of gold, five replacement houris and amnesty in all directions for anybody connected with their cult, and the sultans of the entire Middle East and Persia would at once dispatch anything required.

---

30. **scimitar:** a curved, single-edged sword of Oriental origin.
31. **Old Man of the Mountain:** another name for al-Hasan ibn-al-Sabbah (died 1124), founder of the sect of Assassins.

The sultans were terrified of these heaven-deluded youths who carried out the orders of the cult.

There was no defense against a young man who believed that by assassinating the head of another government he would regain a paradise he had already tasted. That was an unlimited weapon and it all but destroyed the governments of the Middle East. That cult lived for almost three hundred years, the most stable government, if one can call it a government, of the Middle East.

That is a mad story, but history is a parade of madnesses. What if some government, with all the other governments of the world fixated on the idea of atomic fission, developed—just as an extreme example—a weapon called "sleep rain"? This could be a chemical "rain" which would fall over a city and would not hurt anybody, but would put them to sleep. This is certainly not outside the scope of chemical weapons.

Scientists left to their own devices sit around and "dream up" weapons. The weapon mentioned above is one I heard of in a conference of scientists at Western Electric.[32] They had it all worked out—the number of parts and materials to be used—and they were challenging a chemist from a nearby chemical works for the details. One would have thought that they were some grand council for something or other charged with the entire responsibility for annihilating the human race. They decided that constructing sleep rain was feasible, and then lost interest. They all got drunk instead of making the world go to sleep.

An Interim Weapon

Sleep rain might be called an *interim weapon*. It would be very effective because no country can govern its population if

---

32. **Western Electric:** an American electrical company.

they are all asleep. They would simply wake up and find the occupying force sitting in the palace or parliament.

One of the more amazing frames of mind occurs in man when he suddenly finds his citadel[33] invested[34] as he wakes up in the morning. During the war some marines had a similar idea. A group of Japanese suddenly woke up to find that they were all tied up. They couldn't move or go anyplace. They were totally invested. The calmness of the investing force was rather fantastic. They had slipped up on a beach unexpectedly and surrounded the barracks.[35] There wasn't any sentry[36] because that area was so far out of the war zone that they didn't expect any danger from anybody. The Japanese were very friendly and even cooked rice for everybody. It may not look much like a war to us, but they certainly were under control of the investing force.

In other words, the control of the population of a base had changed, which is the end and goal of war.

There are weapons that can be developed. And probably the greatest danger, unknown to the government, is that somebody might develop one. If everybody were spending 99 percent of their national income on atomic fission and somebody were willing to spend a couple of million on some mad weapon like sleep rain, we would be totally caught—and unexpectedly so.

What if someone bombed a city like Cairo or Baghdad with "crows' feet"? Crows' feet are little pins that have four points, and when they are dropped, they land on three spikes and leave

---

33. **citadel:** any strong fortified place; stronghold.
34. **invested:** surrounded with military forces so as to prevent approach or escape; besieged.
35. **barracks:** a building or group of buildings for lodging soldiers.
36. **sentry:** a soldier stationed at a place to stand guard and prevent the passage of unauthorized persons, watch for fires, etc., especially a sentinel stationed at a pass, gate, opening in a defense work, or the like.

the fourth one in the air. It would probably make it awfully hard for anyone to walk through a city if there were crows' feet all over the streets.

If all one wants to do is throw a population out of control and fight some political activity that has to do with governments, why drag the rest of humanity in? Why should anybody get seriously hurt?

For instance, a certain way to destroy the United States government would be simply to introduce to the country a paper worm that would eat up all the paper. It would make it impossible to fight a war!

The facts of the case then, as far as war weapons are concerned, is that they needn't be serious at all. I have read through the private papers of Nikola Tesla[37]—the man who invented alternating current—and he had some interesting ideas about this.

Tesla stated that there was a feasibility of creating a standing electrical wave[38] on one side of Earth that would then appear on the other side of Earth because of the spherical effect of current flows. In other words, if one were to send a tramp steamer[39] down into the South Pacific and have it pump electricity in the ocean—create a standing wave there—all radio communication in Moscow would become static and anything you would want to

---

37. **Nikola Tesla:** (1856–1943) US physicist, electrical engineer and inventor, born in Austria-Hungary. Among his inventions were generators of high-frequency currents and wireless systems of communication and of power transmission.

38. **standing electrical wave:** an electrical wave which, instead of traveling from one point to another, is stationary. This is due to interactions between a wave transmitted down a line and a wave reflected back. If you can imagine an ocean wave which was no longer rolling but was just sitting there peaked, that would be an example of a standing wave. As another example, a vibrating rope tied at one end will produce a standing wave. See the glossary for an illustration of a standing wave.

39. **tramp steamer:** a freight vessel that does not run regularly between fixed ports, but takes a cargo wherever shippers desire.

put on the air would then appear as the only message in Moscow radio stations.

Scientists dream up these weapons, but normally they are thinking in terms of prank.[40] But what if a group of Argentinian scientists were able to create one of these weapons while the rest were entirely fascinated on the subject of atomic fission? We would perhaps wake up one morning and find ourselves part of the Argentinian Empire.

The Second Danger of the Atomic Bomb

So here is the second great danger of the atomic bomb: It paralyzes observation of scientific possibilities in war. In itself it is not a weapon but a no-game condition. It is, then, a personal menace to you and me by concentrating the attention of governments upon itself and leaving us wide open to anything.

Any nation that creates one of these interim weapons, with everybody defending against nothing but atomic bombs, could cast an empire across the face of Earth with the greatest of ease, with no opposition anywhere.

The future of our race depends upon a continued fluid alertness on the part of a government into all branches of science and a complete and continuous good communication line to scientists, such as doctors of medicine, nuclear physicists and Scientologists, to discover what is known, being done and what we can do. Then our answer to the whole problem is that we could tell what could be done scientifically. There *is* something that the governments of Earth can do.

I don't say that anybody will effect this, or that we ourselves will bring any pressure to bear in any direction, but there is one

---

40. **prank:** a trick of an amusing, playful or sometimes malicious nature.

thing that they all can do. And that is *to become more civilized;* they can better their diplomacy and their understanding of man and make real their communication lines amongst nations.

It is in the interest of a government to make the control of any people better, not worse. H-bombs worsen control in peace as well as war. Therefore they are not a weapon that works in the favor of any government on Earth. The answers to world peace are better controls, not hysteria.

Book Two
Chapter Three

Radiation
and
Scientology

Radiation and Scientology

There are a number of things which have been learned in Scientology which directly relate to radiation and the handling of its effects.

We already have data of sufficient importance and reliability to demonstrate that Scientologists, by application of Scientology processing,[1] can very easily nullify many of the dangers presented by a polluted atmosphere, as many of these dangers are of a mental and spiritual nature.[2]

We care very little about whether there is radiation in the atmosphere because a person who is in excellent physical condition does not particularly suffer mentally and thus physically from the effects of radiation. When a person is at a level where his general physical health is good, then worry over radiation in the atmosphere is not, by itself, capable of depressing him into ill health. Radiation is more of a mental than a physical problem, and Scientology handles that.

---

1. **processing:** the application of Dianetics or Scientology processes to someone by a trained auditor. The exact definition of *processing* is: The action of asking a person a question (which he can understand and answer), getting an answer to that question and acknowledging him for that answer. Also called **auditing.**
2. For more information on Scientology processing, read *Scientology: The Fundamentals of Thought* by L. Ron Hubbard.

The factors in Scientology which are most definitely influenced by radiation are the factors which are most definitely influenced by life. When we try to divide a peculiar illness from the general illness of being alive we are at once in conflict with the fact that man is as well as he is well. If each one of the infinite number of factors which can make him ill had to be taken up separately and independently and distinctly with an entirely different treatment, we would discover ourselves with our noses always and forever stuck into the newest and latest disease. We don't do that although we are aware of the latest techniques.

It is an interesting fact that the latest technique always runs out[3] the effects of earlier techniques—and that is why it is the latest technique. We are not studying the latest disease. We are studying a method to eradicate the cures of former times and the nullification of processes which were used earlier.

A technique is as good as it runs out earlier techniques. The technique which runs out, eradicates or even throws into restimulation[4] an older technique is senior to it.

Let's assume that we are treating smallpox.[5] We find at first that we inject a serum which makes the individual's arm swell up, makes him feel ill and feverish. After that he does or doesn't get smallpox.

After further investigation and research we find that we could refine and perfect this technique by giving it orally. This seems to have a good workability. Finally we discover something that has to do with a particular hot bath—if you can imagine such

---

3. **runs out:** erases, causes to disappear.
4. **restimulation:** reactivation of a past memory due to similar circumstances in the present approximating circumstances of the past.
5. **smallpox:** an acute, highly contagious virus disease characterized by prolonged fever, vomiting, and pustular (of a swelling filled with pus) eruptions that often leave pitted scars, or pockmarks, when healed.

a cure—we might find that if we give somebody a hot bath he won't get smallpox.

Of the three techniques, the one which is senior to the others is the one which will run out the other two. It is quite interesting that if the hot bath technique was a good, pervasive, sweeping technique and was a considerable improvement on the other two, when we put the man in the hot bath, he would at once feel sick in his stomach from the pill and his arm would tend to get swollen from the old injection. After that the pill and injection would not trouble him any longer.

Yesterday's Cure Is Today's Disease

That doesn't happen often in physical medicine, but it is not unknown. With the Scientologist we see this phenomenon often during our handling of people. It is highly probable that man has had cures along the developing genetic line which have become the diseases of tomorrow, and if one can solve the factor of the cure that becomes the disease, one is then capable of this kind of curing. This factor has been solved in Scientology.

Alcohol as a Medicine

Let's take alcohol as an example.

Alcohol was once the greatest medicine that man had. It was a wonderful medicine. If anything happened to a man, from snakebite to a love affair, any disease, in fact, one administered alcohol. That was a cure, but now we have alcoholism.

It is interesting that only a century and a half ago the stores of a British man-of-war[6] amounted in terms of cost to more than

6. **man-of-war:** an armed naval vessel; warship.

50 percent alcoholic beverages and less than 50 percent food and other amenities.[7] Alcohol was quite a tremendous thing.

But here is an oddity. Today alcohol makes one tired. It has evidently been laid in on the genetic line to such a degree that it now produces the illness for which it was most used as a remedy—any time one got tired, one took a drink.

We conceive that the genetic blueprint is marching along and that it accumulates experiences. It is definitely in the realm of genetics, but the geneticist[8] has never realized that the experience the body has in one generation may culminate in another generation. Darwin[9] found that if you took horses up to the high country in the Middle East they would grow long hair after a season or two. When they were taken back into the low, hot country, they wouldn't get rid of the long hair for about four generations. It tells us that the genetic line does carry a memory of what has happened. There are many proofs and incidents of this character.

Very few people have added this into the field of medicine, taking it out of the line of natural selection.[10] Today a person may get tired when he takes a drink. In other words, it restimulates that which it was once made to cure. Possibly on the genetic line, sometime or another, and being far-fetched about it, radiation might have been a cure for something. Using this principle that the cure eventually becomes the disease and eventually restimulates the disease it is supposed to cure, I am sure that somewhere

---

7. **amenities:** things that add to one's comfort, convenience or pleasure.
8. **geneticist:** a specialist or expert in genetics, the science of heredity, dealing with resemblances and differences of related organisms resulting from the interaction of their genes and the environment.
9. **Darwin:** Charles Robert (1809–82), English naturalist and author; originated theory of evolution by natural selection.
10. **natural selection:** a process in nature resulting in the survival and perpetuation of only those forms of plant and animal life having certain favorable characteristics that best enable them to adapt to a specific environment.

on the genetic line, radiation was used to cure a bad stomach or skin. Sunbathing was an example of this.

The Sun Is a Ball of Radiation

What is the sun but a ball of radiation? There are photons[11] that come from the sun, but they are hand in glove[12] with a great deal of other radiation. Radiation is all over the atmosphere and always has been. Sunburn is not an overdose of heat but simply radiation.

In early physics textbooks they used to teach that the sun was combusting[13] on hydrogen. They calculated the length of life of the sun on hydrogen, but if that were so one would get a difference in the heat of the sun from year to year because it would be burning out. It was an interesting fact that the sun didn't burn out, so the theory was eventually abandoned and people finally owned up and said that they didn't know why the sun kept on burning. It was only when nuclear physics became dominant in men's thinking that sunlight was explained, and sunlight is now understood to be occasioned by a continuous fusion going on, on a sphere called the sun. Therefore sunburn is a radiation burn.

Sunburn and Radiation Burns

When one looks at people who are burned in an atomic blast such as there was at Hiroshima, one is looking at burns that look very much like sunburn.

For instance, a man was standing with his back to a picket fence. The bomb exploded far back of him and he had sunburn

---

11. **photons:** units of energy having both particle and wave behavior: they have no charge or mass but possess momentum. The energy of light, X-rays, gamma rays, etc., is carried by photons.
12. **hand in glove:** very intimately associated.
13. **combusting:** burning.

where there weren't any pickets. In other words, he got a burn pattern much as one would if one were wearing a bathing suit.

If radiation is drifting around in the air all the time, one is not getting a direct burn, one is getting a sort of continuous, intolerable type of burn which is too imbalanced and the absorption of which one doesn't find healthy. Every person has a great deal of experience with sunburn on the genetic line. And sunburn occasionally causes hives, red flushes, prickliness, an upset stomach and colitis. It will even cause loss of hair. It is something with which we have had experience. Radiation is not new and strange. There is just more of it and it is drifting in the wrong places.

X-rays

We have also had X-rays. X-rays oddly enough have been used as a cure for cancer. A cure for cancer? It must have been in vogue[14] for some time for the excellent reason that X-ray can cause cancer.

The Solution of a Problem

It is no surprise that if one tries to cure something long enough and often enough, it may eventually cause what it is trying to cure. Its effectiveness will diminish.

In other words, the solution of a problem is the problem, not a solution. If one wants no liability in any solution then its solution is the problem.

For example, somebody decides that his wife is mad and he takes her to see a psychiatrist. They put big electrodes[15] on her

---

14. **vogue:** something in fashion, as at a particular time.
15. **electrodes:** conductors through which an electric current enters or leaves a nonmetallic medium.

head, shock her and send her back. What is she suffering from now? She is suffering from being electrocuted. So one day she walks over to the light and as she turns it on it short-circuits, gives her a slight shock and she is crazy all over again. It often happens and it is quite common. They are using electricity in some wild, barbaric manner in some offhanded attempt to cure insanity.

The Solution Is Always the Problem

This business of curing illnesses carries with it the liability of leaving the cure sitting there. Let's say someone cures a disease by running an individual's temperature to 107 degrees Fahrenheit and leaving it there for 48 hours. A few years go by and something is wrong with him. What is wrong with him? Well, he gets hot!

In order to take a person's fixation off a problem, a Scientology auditor[16] will often have the individual conceive of problems of comparable magnitude to the problem. As long as he is fixated on the problem, even if he then solves it, he continues to be fixated on the problem. He has just put a barrier between himself and the problem, but the problem is still there.

One therefore has to raise the individual's tolerance for that type of problem, and the moment that is done, the problem is "solved." In other words, the solution is always the problem. One has to be able to *handle, tolerate* and *confront* the problem. When one cannot confront a problem and one "solves" it completely, he then becomes obsessed with the solution of it.

Let's take a look at how this applies to radiation. People

---

16. **auditor:** a person trained and qualified in applying Dianetics and/or Scientology processes and procedures to individuals for their betterment; called an auditor because *auditor* means "one who listens."

cannot solve it, and they cannot confront it as it is drifting all through the atmosphere. If one has somebody look into space for a while, telling him, "Don't look at *anything*. Just look into space," after a while this person will be in rather poor condition. He will get queasy.

Therefore, if radiation is scattered all through the air and one tells people "Look, it is floating all around in space, but you cannot see it," everybody starts getting queasy.

One can be made to relive a past experience and therefore can be made to relive past illnesses as *Dianetics:*[17] *The Modern Science of Mental Health* has demonstrated. One can actually see people stuck in these moments of illnesses.

If a person is liable to get restimulated or is upset by dangers in the atmosphere, he will get sick in his stomach a short while after one has asked him to look into space. One gets colitis and gastroenteritis often as a result of this apparently harmless technique of asking people to look into space without paying particular notice to any specific objects that may be present. This is a test anybody could make.

Pollution of Spaces Makes Effect[18] out of Man

Pollution of and danger in space makes a total effect out of man and one is brought to believe one can do nothing about it. These are the combinations from a Scientologist's viewpoint

---

17. **Dianetics:** Dianetics spiritual healing technology. It addresses and handles the effects of the spirit on the body and can alleviate such things as unwanted sensations and emotions, accidents, injuries and psychosomatic illnesses (ones that are caused or aggravated by mental stress). *Dianetics* means "through the soul" (from Greek *dia,* through, and *nous,* soul). It is further defined as "what the soul is doing to the body."

18. **effect:** a point of receipt of flow (thought, energy or action). For example: If one considers a river flowing to the sea, the place where it began would be the source-point or cause, the place where it went into the sea would be the effect-point, and the sea would be the effect of the river. A man firing a gun is cause; a man receiving a bullet is effect.

which bring about this condition we know as radiation sickness, and we can do something about each one of them. We can give man something to confront that is like radiation and being able to confront this we give him practice in confronting the unconfrontable.

None of this, however, nullifies the actual physical danger of radiation which *does* bring about a *physical* deterioration.

The Other Factors behind Radiation

What are the other factors behind radiation? Radiation is being used as a control mechanism. It is being used to control people. They are not supposed to have war with and are to obey countries that do have radiation.

As it goes on it becomes apparent to people that it is a control mechanism.

Control

As long as a person is allergic to control, he will suffer from attempts to control him. If he has an allergy to control and to being controlled and thinks that there is something wrong with control, that is an aberration. It is something that should be handled by a Scientologist to raise the person's tolerance of it. People get so afraid of being controlled that they resist everything. When radiation is used as a control mechanism, they resist it and it burns them—and only then does it burn them.

Resistance to Control

A person can only be controlled against his will as long as he is allergic to control and it is against his will. A person who is very bland about this subject and doesn't mind being controlled can be controlled as easily as a toy and can stop the control as easily as a giant. He has power of choice over control, and if one has power of choice over control it doesn't much matter if one is being controlled or controlling a situation or persons oneself.

As long as control, directions, orders and postulates[19] are resisted, a person has a tendency to lock up with them—in other words, become their effect, which then produces a considerable discomfort to the person. Resistance to a terminal[20] brings about, one way or another, a closure of terminals[21] with the thing to such a degree that an individual then obeys it and doesn't know he is obeying it or what he is obeying. And that is more or less what aberration is.[22]

Radiation and Control

If radiation is used as a control factor then a person is made to close terminals with[23] something which his body cannot tolerate. But it is the *person* who is closing that terminal, *not* the body, and that is our foremost discovery. As long as we have an orientation on the subject of radiation, are no longer mentally resisting it or upset about it, and particularly if we are in fair condition with regard to space and spaciousness and don't get claustrophobia,[24] then we really don't have to fear radiation as a control factor. That is the first thing that was learned in Scientology about radiation.

Scientologists know a great deal about radiation since a

---

19. **postulates:** conclusions, decisions or resolutions made by the individual himself to resolve a problem or set a pattern for the future or nullify a pattern of the past.
20. **terminal:** something that has mass and meaning; a point from which energy can flow or by which energy can be received.
21. **closure of terminals:** the phenomenon of terminals (people, fixed masses, etc.) collapsing into each other or becoming identified, one with the other.
22. For further information on this phenomenon, read the book *Dianetics 55!* by L. Ron Hubbard.
23. **close terminals with:** to collapse into or identify oneself with something.
24. **claustrophobia:** an abnormal fear of being in enclosed or narrow places.

Scientology organization was once located in Arizona, 250 miles from the site of over a hundred atomic bomb tests that were made in Nevada. The central headquarters of this organization was moved from Phoenix, Arizona, to Washington, DC, only because pianos began to count like uranium mines. Everything was live and radioactive. Dust blew in one's face at night and one had sunburn although there was no sun. There was just too much radiation.

We had a lot of experience and found something rather peculiar. We found that people who were in good condition were not bothered with regard to radiation and those who were in bad condition would get sick in their stomachs from something that would hardly count on a Geiger counter.[25] Those people received Scientology processing and had no further repercussion from radiation.

Here is a good example. A man came into the Hubbard Scientology Organization in Phoenix. He had been driving past one of the atomic bomb explosion sites, and as he went past the site at some considerable distance away, he saw the flash on the horizon. At once his face and eyes swelled and he could hardly drive into Phoenix. He was in terrible condition and felt very bad about this. So I just gave him a Scientology assist[26] and the swelling went down immediately.

General auditing[27] of individuals is then a basic solution.

---

25. **Geiger counter:** an instrument used for detecting and measuring radioactivity; named after H. Geiger (1882–1945), German physicist.

26. **assist:** processing which assists the individual to heal himself or be healed by another agency by removing his reasons for precipitating (bringing on) and prolonging his condition and lessening his predisposition (inclination or tendency) to further injure himself or remain in an intolerable condition.

27. **auditing:** another word for *processing*, the application of Dianetics or Scientology processes to someone by a trained auditor. *See also* **processing** in the glossary.

Group auditing[28] also solves the control factor and helps communication to a marked degree.

Nutrition and Radiation

The reaction to radiation in persons who have been given Scientology processing is by actual test much lower than those who have not received it. We have conducted some experiments in that direction. However, one still has to care for the physical body and its reactions on a biochemical level.

Is there anything that we could give a person that would help him against radiation? There is. There are several preparations which prevent radiation sickness. It is getting rather common now and progress is being made on the whole subject.

Several researchers have found that harmful effects of radiation can be reduced by injecting some quite simple chemicals before exposure to the rays.

A short time ago such a suggestion would have been thought absurd. Today chemical protection against radiation is a subject of much research.

Dianazene[29]

We have been leading on this. I conducted several experiments in 1950 which were in total disagreement with the pharmacopeia,[30] but any medical doctor or biochemist could make the

---

28. **group auditing:** Scientology auditing techniques administered to groups of children or adults.

29. **Dianazene:** a formula combining nicotinic acid with other vitamins and minerals which was developed to make the intake of nicotinic acid more effective in handling radiation.

30. **pharmacopeia:** an authoritative book containing a list and description of drugs and medicinal products together with the standards established under law for their production, dispensation, use, etc.

same experiments. One would administer 200 mg of nicotinic acid[31] (also called *niacin*) per day to somebody and see all the manifestations I have mentioned earlier turn on,[32] eventually disappear and not recur until one has administered about 500 mg per day, which will turn it all on again, but much less this time. Then one gives this person 1,000 mg per day for several days and finds that there is just a small reaction, after which one administers 2,000 mg per day and finds no more effects.

So we knew that old-time nicotinic acid restimulated and ran out sunburns, and that a person who had been given nicotinic acid actually did not receive a continuous effect from it.

Thus it happens that there is an incorrect entry in both the British and American pharmacopeias. It says that nicotinic acid— not niacinamide[33]—turns on a flush, and an overdose is therefore toxic. This is not correct.

It is fascinating that there could be this insufficient information. It could be that people don't look, because that isn't what it does at all. In a large number of cases it doesn't turn on flushes but turns on hives, gastroenteritis, aching bones, or a fearful, terrified condition which is not a physical reaction at all. Here is a variable reaction from something "toxic"—and notice that it turns on the conditions brought about by atomic radiation.

What sort of a toxic pill is this which when administered over a period of time is no longer toxic, even though all the time it is being administered it is above toleration? The body cannot

---

31. **nicotinic acid:** same as **niacin.** *See* **niacin** in the glossary.
32. **turn on:** start suddenly to affect or show.
33. **niacinamide:** a form of niacin invented by the medical profession to avoid the flush which is turned on when a person takes niacin. What the medical profession didn't realize was that niacin itself doesn't turn on a flush—the flush is caused by the fact that sunburn or radiation is being run out. Niacinamide is worthless for the purpose of running out radiation.

tolerate the amount that is being administered but after a while it no longer has any effect. Unless one knows Dianetics and Scientology this doesn't seem to make much sense.

Nicotinic acid apparently runs out or abolishes sunburns, and that is the simple answer to this question. When it is given to a person, he gets sunburns he has already had before and turns as red as a beet. Keep him on a regimented dose every day and after a while two things can happen: One, he no longer gets sick when nicotinic acid is administered to him; and two, he doesn't have a bad reaction from sunburn.

We have made the test with sunlamps and found that a person's liability to being burned is decreased by the administration of nicotinic acid and the running out of past burns. This, therefore, is true of this type of radiation illness.

Remembering that series of experiments I made in 1950 I again looked them up in the files. We later got some brave volunteers who took nicotinic acid over a period of a couple of weeks and sure enough our old experiments were bearing out with one exception: The reactions per dose were five and six times more violent than they had been in 1950!

I then got hold of some of the people who were given nicotinic acid in 1950 and they took the same regimen all over again. They got a little sick in their stomachs but were better off than other people, and they got an entirely different reaction.

In order to make the intake of nicotinic acid more effective, I did more experimenting and eventually combined it with other vitamins and minerals and finally produced a formula called Dianazene.

The Formula for Dianazene

Nicotinic acid	200 milligrams
Iron—Ferrous Gluconate[34]	10 grains
Vitamin B$_1$[35]	25 milligrams
Vitamin B$_2$[36]—Riboflavin	50 milligrams
Vitamin C—Ascorbic Acid	200 to 500 milligrams
Dicalcium Phosphate[37]	15 to 20 grains

Observation in research indicated that it should be taken daily, all at the same time, with milk and chocolate.

It is not the best solution. But if we didn't have anything else, Dianazene might serve the purpose very well in a limited sense.

Research has shown that Dianazene apparently runs out radiation—or what appears to be radiation. It also appears to proof a person up against the effects of radiation to some degree.

Dianazene has been seen to run out what appeared to be skin cancer. A man who didn't have much liability to skin cancer (he only had a few moles) took Dianazene. His whole jaw turned into a raw mass of cancer. He kept on taking Dianazene and it disappeared after a while. We were looking at a case of cancer that might have happened.

---

34. **ferrous gluconate:** a type of iron supplement compound, containing considerably more absorbable iron than other types.
35. **vitamin B$_1$:** a vitamin, also called thiamine, important to the body in the functions of cell oxidation (respiration), growth, carbohydrate metabolism, stimulation and transmission of nerve impulses, etc.
36. **vitamin B$_2$:** also called riboflavin, a vitamin important in the metabolism of protein and in skin, liver and eye health.
37. **dicalcium phosphate:** a substance consisting of calcium and phosphorus used as a mineral supplement in the Dianazene formula.

There was another instance of somebody who had a little bit of colitis which worried him slightly from time to time. After taking Dianazene he started to bleed from the intestines. He kept on taking this formula and came out apparently without colitis. He may have been facing an eventual colitis of a fatal nature—hemorrhages.

The whole point in taking Dianazene was to keep taking it until bad effects vanished.

As the level of food intake from country to country varies, it is important that people who don't eat regular wholesome food take milk and chocolate with this preparation. Otherwise they get a very poor reaction to it. I found that if one took milk and chocolate with it—or milk and glucose—it worked much better. In other words, the people who are the poorest fed would evidently be the most susceptible to radiation.

However, there could be thousands of other factors involved. If we are alert there is no reason to worry about radiation at this time particularly. But there is a worry about the case[38] and health level of the peoples of the Earth, and if we continue along in this same direction, we would also win in the face of radiation. Who knows that we wouldn't get a plague tomorrow that would wipe out nations. I assure you that it would be the people who are worried and are in a bad state of health who would go down first.

If one wanted to get the better of the plague, whether man- or bug-made, one should be audited by Scientology technologies. That seems to me about all I could say offhand that one might find of use in the understanding and handling of atomic radiation.

---

38. **case:** a person's mental condition. A person's *case* is the way he responds to the world around him by reason of his aberrations.

Book Two
Chapter Four

Man's Real Enemies

Man's Real Enemies

The whole subject of atomic fission is a subject of violence. It isn't true that every new scientific development carries with it violence, but atomic fission does, because its first use was in war for the slaughter of men, women and children at Hiroshima. It has carried with it a considerable reputation, but the position of Scientologists is very sharp and clear. I have covered the two important factors which I will mention again.

Point number one is: *The first danger of atomic fission and the testing of bombs is the hysteria it can cause amongst populaces, a hysteria which can grow so great that a populace can be thrown out of control;* and point number two: *The people who suffer from small doses of radiation are people who have a bad health record,* who are not in excellent mental and physical condition.

It is possible to take somebody who is in excellent mental and physical condition and give him enough dosage to make him extremely ill, but per the studies done on this, the people who are affected the most by radiation are the infirm,[1] the old, those who are liable to various shocks and upsets in life anyway.

This factor has not been covered by atomic energy releases

---

1. **infirm:** feeble or weak in body and in health, especially because of age; ailing.

since it is not much investigated except by ourselves. Therefore, concluding the second point, those people who are in excellent condition and whose mental stability is beyond question, need have less fear of the effects of radiation in the environment.

Under the heading of number one, a Scientologist by group auditing is capable of bringing a considerable calmness into an area which is upset, and under point number two, it is the business of a Scientologist to place people into a level of existence where they don't get sick from every stray germ that wanders their way. This is one of our goals. Therefore these two points are completely germane to Scientology.

The Harmful Effects of X-rays

X-rays are fully as deadly as atomic fission. A repeated continuous application of X-rays to a person can bring about anything and everything that atomic fission can cause through pollution of the atmosphere. It certainly brings about a condition of high radiation count in the individual if many X-rays are taken, so that if he gets a little more X-ray or radiation fallout, he is liable to become ill. Yet X-rays are ordinarily applied to sick people!

The Genetic Aspects of the Atomic Bomb

As far as the genetic aspects of the atomic bomb are concerned, this is, of course, where everybody's attention centers, because sex is still so secret in Anglo-American society. It is a good thing that we are not living in Victorian times, because we would not dare mention the fact that our children could be born with their legs coming out of their ears. It is still sufficiently secret to pin people's attention to the genetic aspects of radiation. These are of least importance and are of no great consequence at this time.

The mortality rate of babies a century ago because of puerperal fever[2] was, by percentage, a hundred times higher than is the rate of deformities due to radiation. The percentage of deformities and blindness caused by bad midwifery and poor medical practice a century and a half ago surpasses the radiation figures and if anybody wants to be shocked about it, let him be shocked about the way it was then, not the way it is going to be. Of course, it is upsetting to think of a hundred million populace having several thousand congenital idiots simply because of nuclear contamination. But how about the people who are already born and grown up who will become ill, ineffective and die? That is a more important fact. Testing *at its present rate* isn't going to spoil completely the genetic line.

I was visiting a hospital some time ago and came across a girl who had had a baby about ten to twelve days before. She had stayed several days beyond when they would ordinarily have dismissed her. She was lying in a very inert position, looking very sad. I asked her doctor what the matter was and he told me that something had happened during the pregnancy. The baby was all right, but only half the placenta[3] developed. This was a malformation and the woman believed that something was wrong with her due to this development of the placenta. This so deprived her of her usual spirits that she lay there not recovering.

I became very interested in this as I knew that X-rays disarrange the genes,[4] and the placenta is represented in the genes. If one of these genes is deranged, one can get such things as half a placenta.

I was thinking in terms of all the radiation that was in this

---

2. **puerperal fever:** a poisoned state of the birth canal and the bloodstream occurring at childbirth. Also called childbed fever.
3. **placenta:** an organ that develops in the womb during pregnancy and supplies the fetus with nourishment.
4. **genes:** any of the units occurring at specific points on the chromosomes by which specific hereditary characters are passed on to the next generation.

area, as they were blowing up bomb after bomb about 250 miles away. Theoretically, it could have been those bombs that were causing her genetic upset.

So I asked her, "What does your husband do?" thinking possibly that he was one of the people who was associated with the tests. She told me, however, that he was a radiologist, an X-ray technician. I then asked her what duty he was performing nine months earlier, and after a while she groaned her answer which was that her husband was taking a special course of training on new X-ray equipment at a certain military hospital nearby and for six days had been doing nothing else but setting up and using the most powerful X-ray equipment extant.

This woman fortunately was well educated, and I said, "Did it ever occur to you that it might not be your fault that only half a placenta developed?" From that moment her interest in life returned and she left the hospital that afternoon, unable to wait to confront her husband with this discovery.

It seemed probable that the testing of atomic bombs 250 miles away did not cause the disarrangement in the case of this particular woman. Her husband, being an X-ray technician, had been on a spree of X-ray training and his own genes may have been badly disarranged by the X-ray equipment and his use of it.

People tend to pick out an assumed cause for something and blame it for all that cannot otherwise be explained satisfactorily. Radiation is loose in the world and everything then is assigned to radiation. People do this fixedly.

Wrong Assignment of Cause

Many more things should be assigned to radiation at this moment than are being assigned to it. People are not at all aware of the tremendous effect that radiation has and the low morale that it will give people.

However, people will assign more and more things to radiation, and just about the time when they are assigning about enough, somebody will say that they must not do so and prohibit them from doing so. They will obsessively start assigning things to it until somebody starts jailing people for causing hysteria. After that, people will start misassigning and assigning in a dispersed manner anything to everything, and it will no longer make sense. People will no longer be capable of assigning actual cause, and then there will be chaos.

The thing to do is to be factual about it and say that just certain things are assignable to radiation. Assign them, take them in stride and the government will do extremely well to work along with organizations such as the Scientologist. One should do what one can about them. Publish this data rather widely, showing that the necessary steps that can be taken are being taken, and be factual about it the whole way. One shouldn't try to play it down but should be factual and go on from there, trying to do something not only about radiation but also about the many things that make life all but impossible for people. Shortage of food can be much more fatal than alarm on radiation.

Man's First Enemy Is Man

First among man's enemies is man, because man does more in one war than all the bugs of Africa have ever done.

Man's inhumanity to man was a subject which was addressed with the philosophy of Jesus of Nazareth. But Christianity has not stopped war. It has done a lot of good in this world but it has not stopped war. Unless man can stop this international insanity one will see this thing called radiation—the hydrogen bomb and the guided missile—used by some country against us all and itself at the same time.

It is all very well to say that nobody will use nuclear weapons. Just about the time when somebody is losing a war—up to that time they were being gentlemen and were only killing each other with steel-jacketed bullets—some Herr Hitler or somebody of that ilk will say, "Press button *A*." Button *A* is wired up to a lot of guided missiles and requires only one man's decision to destroy an entire continent, to poison the atmosphere so thoroughly that man vanishes from this planet.

The Real Danger

The real danger is not radiation. The true danger is man's uncivilized state. Unless something can come along and cure him of his barbarism, he is not going to survive. He has many enemies, if he really wants enemies. The locust of Africa, the various fevers of India and the hail storms of Kansas are enemies. Why focus on radiation? If man is to survive he must first be capable of facing his enemies—and those enemies aren't man. He just thinks they are. Until man can be brought to face his true enemies on Earth, he cannot really be considered to be a civilized being, because he is fighting the wrong targets.

The Worthwhile Projects Are Neglected Because of War

How man, making such slow progress on every other frontier, can waste time to turn around and fight his brother is appalling. The Sahara desert could be put under cultivation and that would straighten out some of the economic situations in that area. This would require much less effort than was put into the North African campaigns.[5] It would have to be carefully planned. Man already was making progress in this direction before World War II came into being and retarded the little progress he had already made.

One cannot keep overrunning an area with the terror of war

---

5. **North African campaigns:** a series of battles between Germany and Great Britain during World War II, fought in the desert of North Africa.

and its destruction and decide that anything is going to survive in that area. Man has a madness and that madness is called war. That madness really hasn't anything to do with politics.

Most people who go into a long chant about how one outlaws war are saying that we must suppress national governments. That is the last thing I would ever advise. The truth is very simple. A government becomes worried about its ability to control its populace and neighbors and resorts to war as a means of compelling obedience at home as well as abroad.

In actuality, a weakness and insecurity of government causes war. If a government were very strong and felt very secure, it would employ the most peaceful, quiet methods of granting beingness[6] and getting cooperation from its potential enemies. It wouldn't fight a war. One doesn't find an educated, secure man fighting with his neighbors. No, the person who fights his neighbors is a very insecure and not at all sane man.

War Begets War

To bring about peace, it is not enough to suppress and smash down every single government in the world. That is just emotion in the wrong direction. That is how wars are caused. After the blood bath of the French Revolution, France was in a continuous war for decades. In other words, she was fairly well at peace as long as she had a king and a fairly strong government.

---

6. **granting beingness:** the ability or willingness to let someone else be what he is. *Beingness* is defined as the assumption of a category of identity. An example of beingness would be one's own name. Another example would be one's profession. Another example would be one's physical characteristics. Each or all of these things could be called one's beingness. Beingness is assumed by oneself or given to oneself, or is attained. For example, in the playing of a game each player has his own beingness. Listening to what someone has to say and taking care to understand them, being courteous, refraining from needless criticism, expressing admiration or affinity are examples of the actions of someone who can grant others beingness. The ability to grant others beingness is one of the highest virtues one can have.

When that government was turned over to Robespierres[7] and Napoleons, there was a continuous state of war.

To have nullified the tremendous wasteful efforts of France and all the suffering which pursued those various wars, it would have been necessary to bolster the French government, not weaken it. As long as every nation is upset about every other nation and as long as any nation refuses to bolster and strengthen its neighbor nations, then war remains a threat.

If the United States were willing to grant beingness to the various other great nations of the world and if they were willing to grant beingness to her, one would see a security mounting up which would practically make war impossible.

The Trouble with Russia

The trouble with Russia is that its government is weak. Its government has been overthrown by revolution and has been a threat to world peace ever since, just as France became an international menace in 1790. The Russian Revolution never should have happened. But the conditions of Russia never should have happened either. In other words, the noncivilized condition of Russia, its unenlightened state for the last many centuries directly resulted in this threat we call Russia today.

Regardless of any political philosophy, unless Russia and its satellites can prosper in one way or the other, they will continue to be a "have not" nation.

The Answer to the Atomic Bomb

The answer to the atomic bomb does not lie in the field of "there shall be no further development in the field of the atomic

---

7. **Robespierres:** persons similar to Maximilien Robespierre (1758–94), one of the leaders of the French Revolution whose name is closely associated with the 2,500 people who were guillotined during the Revolution.

bomb." We all know that if a war weapon exists it will be used some time. *The answer to the atomic bomb lies in the change of status of man and his national governments.* These governments must be stronger and people must cooperate with them. They must be strengthened and the peoples of those nations must be addressed realistically and brought up to a point where they can feel some security, where they can *have* something and exist themselves at peace with their own neighbors, and only then have we solved the problem of the atomic bomb. All the atomic bomb is doing is catalyzing the necessity for this solution.

If a technology exists which can bring a higher level of civilization to man, then that technology should be used to the utmost to advance that state of civilization. It should not be used to destroy or decry governments, to propagandize or pull the rug out from underneath the men who are trying. It should be used to bring about stronger, more secure governments and more civilized populaces.

The Turn of the Road

We are at a turn of the road. Man before could almost afford to go into a state of barbarism. Today he cannot afford his bestiality, his inhumanity to his neighbors, for many reasons—not the least of which is that the next war will be the last war. One really shouldn't worry about the next war. It will be over in twenty minutes. But we should try to make that war unnecessary.

The Use of Technology

Man's technology has to be put to a use which will *benefit* civilization. This includes creating sources of cheap power and applying the knowledge we have gained to make industry more efficient. People sometimes worry about automation, as they worry that too much automation will throw them out of work. But if people work, they must have something to buy. There must be something to buy for the money one possesses as money is just as good as one can buy something with it and as bad as one cannot.

Money is something that can be converted into product. Supposing one had a workman's idea of a wonderful civilization whereby everybody did piecework[8] all by himself and was paid abundantly for it. What is he going to do with this great amount of money if he cannot buy piecework which is not available?

A workman certainly ought to have a radio, a decent home well furnished. His children ought to have good clothes and there ought to be wholesome food on the table. He should have a motor car to take him places. He believes this whether he is a Spaniard, Frenchman or American. But if these commodities don't get manufactured in sufficient numbers to make them cheap, nobody is going to have them, and that is a point which he overlooks. Automation must be present in this society. There must be something that can produce enough so man can have enough.

Our present society is existing on a small percent of its workers. The potential workers in society are being diverted in many directions on a nonproductive level, such as war weapons. Every time one builds war weapons one has just expended workers and everything it takes to support these workers. One has to have automation in order to make up for the loss.

If a nation is going to be successful, it has got to have raw products, fuel and willing workers. Get short of one of these three and it will not be successful.

The Willing Worker

The South American nations have more raw products and more fuel, but less willing workers than most nations, and you

---

8. **piecework:** work done and paid for by the piece.

see some South American people still running around in loin-cloths and carrying bows and arrows. These countries have the fuel and raw materials but not the willing workers.

If all the workmen in America and England became unwilling to work, one would again see a barbarism. We in Scientology could prevent such unwillingness rather easily. We have taken that up and solved it in *The Problems of Work.*[9]

One can orient a person with regard to work and make him brace up to it and have a good time whereas he has been avoiding work before. In other words, we can restore his lost willingness. If anything will kill Western society, it is either tremendous political blunders which bring about an atomic war, or this philosophy that work is too hard to confront. This philosophy of "we must all retire some day" amounts to "our greatest ambition is to do nothing." That idea is one of our greatest enemies.

This is how this state of mind is created: A man is having a good time building, let us say, a bird cage. Somebody comes along and says to him, "Aren't you tired? You're working so hard. I should think that after a long day at the office you would feel worn out and would be incapable of going on any further." This man was enjoying building a bird cage. The next day somebody criticizes him at the office about his work and he feels tired.

Tiredness is willingness gone bad. People who are willing don't get tired. It is only when something makes man unwilling, stops him too often and kills his interest in what he is doing that he becomes exhausted.

People have to be told and kept in the frame of mind that life

---

9. *The Problems of Work:* a book by L. Ron Hubbard on the subject of work. This contains solutions to the basic difficulties associated with work, such as overcoming exhaustion, the secrets of efficiency, handling confusing situations and much more.

is worth living and that things are worth doing. If governments and civilizations continue to produce things to convince people that they are just slaves and that things aren't worth doing and that they have to be pushed into work with a whip, the whole society degenerates.

No society can exist on a fabric of slaves. Those that have, have died: Greece, Rome, Germany. A society can only survive when it is built by the shoulders and hands of willing men. Governments should take this into account. They do with social security, health programs, etc., but they can do more about it.

These things are more important than radiation. Man's inhumanity to man has always been present. He has always been able to reach over and put his hand on a deadly and diabolical[10] weapon. Whether that weapon was a club with a knot at the end of it, a tower musket,[11] a new high-powered, super-velocity bazooka,[12] or a guided missile with an atomic bomb in it, remember that it was handled by a man who was being inhuman to men. Therefore the solving of the atomic bomb would not prevent atomic warfare.

Helping the Governments of Earth

A government will always accept a helping hand, but it is so scarce that it takes a government leader a long time to be convinced that it is being held out. So few people help the government that they don't know what the hand is out for. Men use governments to feather their own nests[13] and better their own

---

10. **diabolical:** having the qualities of a devil; fiendish; outrageously wicked.

11. **tower musket:** a firearm of the sixteenth century. It was very long and heavy and had to be rested on a post on the ground for support when in use.

12. **bazooka:** a weapon of metal tubing, for aiming and launching electrically fired, armor-piercing rockets.

13. **feather their own nests:** obtain money, ethically or unethically, for themselves; obtain money or an unfair share of money from the efforts of others; provide for oneself with no regard to the welfare of others.

---

ends, but there are sincere men in government who are trying to do what is right.

If we wish to go any direction in the field of politics let's be sure we go in the direction of giving the existing governments and the powers that be a hand in bringing about a higher level of civilization and a better understanding of life. If we strike at anything, we should strike at these intermediate problems such as the atomic bomb, smallpox, whooping cough,[14] bubonic plague[15] and all the rest of the things that confront man as his enemies.

What do we have in Scientology with which to help man and governments? We have something which assists man, not something that fights man's enemies. Man will fight his real enemies which he isn't fighting now.

Our job as Scientologists in this society is to bring man up to a level where he can confront his natural enemies and live at peace with his fellows, and if we can do that on a very broad level as we are doing in a smaller sphere, then we would have brought a better civilization to Earth.

And that, I think, is what we are trying to do.

Conclusion

The interests of Scientology in radiation are only these:

It creates widespread hysteria;
Scientology can handle hysteria.

---

14. **whooping cough:** an infectious bacterial disease usually of children, characterized by inflammation of the air passages, with convulsive fits of coughing that end with a loud, gasping sound (whoop).

15. **bubonic plague:** a very dangerous contagious disease, accompanied by fever, chills and swelling of the lymphatic glands. It is carried to humans by fleas from rats or squirrels.

It creates physical disabilities;
Scientology can help prevent them.

Scientology is the principle agency that is helping to prevent radiation disabilities in people at this time.

The radiation count of Earth has not been increased by bomb testing. The anguish of Earth has been multiplied by bomb terror. You can survive with Scientology.

Book Two
Chapter Five

Handling the Cumulative
Effects of Radiation:

The Purification
Program

Handling the Cumulative Effects of Radiation: The Purification Program

The material in the preceding chapters was written in 1957.

This chapter gives the results of research done in the 1970s, making breakthroughs in the field of detoxification and refining the original discoveries on the effects of accumulated radiation.

The Cumulative Effects of Radiation

Atomic war has been more or less neglected as a news subject since the late fifties. But that doesn't make it any less a threat. All it takes is one psychopath[1] politician with access to the war-peace button. And today there are a dozen or more atomic-armed nations.

Further, the increased use of atomic power for electrical supply (without developing proper technology and safeguards in its use) poses a nonmilitary threat.

And the deterioration of the upper atmosphere of the planet, by jets and pollutants, is year by year letting more and more sun radiation through to the planetary surface.

---

1. **psychopath:** a person whose behavior is largely amoral and asocial and who is characterized by irresponsibility, lack of remorse or shame, perverse or impulsive (often criminal) behavior and other serious personality defects, generally without psychotic attacks or symptoms.

Radiation causes a cumulative effect. The more one is exposed to radiation, the less resistance he has and the more effect the radiation has on him. In other words, a build-up occurs.

The problem then becomes how to rid a person of the effects of *past* exposures to radiation.

The first clues to the solution came with the Dianazene research done in the '50s. With further research and testing, a program was developed which apparently handles not only the effects of radiation exposure, but also the residual effects of drugs and other toxins. This is called the *Purification* program.

The Purification Program

The primary purpose of the Purification program is to handle drugs and toxic substances accumulated in the body, and, according to the success stories pouring in, it certainly does that.[2]

The Purification program is a tightly supervised regimen, including the following elements:

Exercise, in the form of outside running, to stimulate the circulation.

Prescribed periods in a sauna, which, accompanied by certain vitamins and other nutrients, enable one to sweat out the accumulated toxins.

A properly ordered personal schedule which provides the person with a normal eight hours of sleep.

A nutritional program, including:

One's regular diet which is then supplemented with

2. For the full theory and an exact description of the application of this program, read the book *Clear Body, Clear Mind: The Effective Purification Program*, by L. Ron Hubbard.

plenty of fresh vegetables which are not overcooked.

Sufficient liquids to offset the loss of body fluids in sweating.

An exact regimen of vitamin, mineral and oil intake.

Niacin is an important element of the vitamins used during this program and increasing amounts are used throughout, always kept in balance with other vitamins and minerals.

Because quantities of niacin are taken and because of the heat of the sauna, the Purification program apparently can have the effect of running out a certain amount—possibly not all—of the radiation in people.

Further, radiation is apparently enormously water soluble as well as water movable. According to researchers, one merely has to take a hose to a building surface or road to wash the radiation off of it. This factor is well known to defense-trained personnel. So the generally large quantities of liquid taken in and then sweated out while on the program may also contribute to the reduction of accumulated radiation.

Niacin

One of the parts of the Purification program is *niacin*. The discoveries I made with this vitamin in the '50s began with its apparent effect on radiation exposure. At that time there was a lot of bomb testing and general radiation exposure and we had lots and lots of people who had been subjected to atomic tests, atomic accidents and, in at least one case, to materials that had been part of an old atomic explosion. We were engaged in salvaging these people and we succeeded.

Niacin seems to have a catalytic effect on running out radiation exposure. It seems to give it a kick and run it through. It will often cause a very hot flush and prickly, itchy skin, which can last up to an hour or longer. It may also bring on chills or make one feel tired.

However, if one continues niacin—always along with other necessary vitamins in proper amounts—any bad effects vanish.

Program Results

From its earliest application and pilot programs, people on the Purification program reported experiencing, in mild form, some of the sensations of old sunburns and X-ray exposures, radioactive contaminations and some of the illnesses, injuries and emotional conditions that went with them.

These same persons also reported the apparent exudation[3] of substances smelling or tasting or feeling like street drugs, medicines, anesthetics, diet pills, food preservatives, pesticides and any number of other chemical preparations in common use.

However, where the person was on a sensible and well-kept schedule and taking correct nutrient dosages, and all other parts of the program were followed, the manifestations associated with the residues of these substances would deintensify and disappear without hanging up and without undue discomfort for the person.

When the program was fully completed, people reported no longer feeling the effects of these contaminations or impurities going into restimulation. To the contrary, they reported a marked resurgence of overall well-being!

---

3. **exudation:** the action of coming out gradually in drops, as sweat, through pores or small openings; oozing out.

Purification and Man's Future

As radiation's effects appear to be cumulative, it follows that if one were able to get rid of the cumulative effects of it, one would be far less subject to new blasts of it. While one would not be made wholly immune to new incidents, he would be far less affected by them.

Completely aside from the physical resurgence experienced in the Purification program when properly and fully done, there is this side-benefit of lessening the consequences of future radiation exposure.

Bombarded by radiation from atomic plant fallout, from lessened atmospheric protection, people today are far more subject to being victims in the time of atomic war. The cumulative effect of radiation has set them up to a rapid demise in the face of heavy atomic fallout.

That brings us to the interesting probability that those who have had a full and competent Purification program will survive, where others not so fortunate won't.

And *that* poses the interesting possibility that only Scientologists will be functioning in areas experiencing heavy atomic fallout in an atomic war.

And they'll know how to recover from a new exposure— another short use of niacin. And a bit of auditing, of course.

About the Author

About the Author

L. Ron Hubbard is one of the most acclaimed and widely read authors of all time, primarily because his works express a firsthand knowledge of the nature of man—knowledge gained not from standing on the sidelines but through lifelong experience with people from all walks of life.

As Ron said, "One doesn't learn about life by sitting in an ivory tower, thinking about it. One learns about life by being part of it." And that is how he lived.

He began his quest for knowledge on the nature of man at a very early age. When he was eight years old he was already well on his way to being a seasoned traveler. His adventures included voyages to China, Japan and other points in the Orient and South Pacific, covering a quarter of a million miles by the age of nineteen. In the course of his travels he became closely acquainted with twenty-one different races all over the world.

In the fall of 1930, Ron pursued his studies of mathematics and engineering, enrolling at George Washington University where he was also a member of one of the first American classes on nuclear physics. He realized that neither the East nor the West contained the full answer to the problems of existence. Despite all of mankind's advances in the physical sciences, a *workable* technology of the mind and life had never been developed. The mental "technologies" which did exist, psychology and psychiatry, were actually barbaric, false subjects—no more workable than the methods of jungle witch doctors. Ron shouldered the responsibility of filling this gap in the knowledge of mankind.

He financed his early research through fiction writing. He became one of the most highly demanded authors in the golden age of popular adventure and science fiction writing during the 1930s and 1940s, interrupted only by his service in the US Navy during World War II.

Partially disabled at the war's end, Ron applied what he had learned from his researches. He made breakthroughs and developed techniques which made it possible for him to recover from his injuries and help others to regain their health. It was during this time that the basic tenets of Dianetics technology were codified. Part of his early research into the nature of mental phenomena included a study of the endocrine system and effect of the mind on the body's ability to absorb and use nutrients.

In 1947, he wrote a manuscript detailing his discoveries. It was not published at that time, but circulated amongst Ron's friends, who copied it and passed it on to others. (This manuscript was formally published in 1951 as *Dianetics: The Original Thesis* and later republished as *The Dynamics of Life*.) The interest generated by this manuscript prompted a flood of requests for more information on the subject.

Ron provided all his discoveries to the American Psychiatric Association and the American Medical Association. Despite the fact that his work would have benefited them and society immensely, they ignored his research and continued on with their archaic activities.

Meanwhile, the steadily increasing flow of letters asking for further information and requesting that he detail more applications of his new subject resulted in Ron spending all his time answering letters. He decided to write and publish a comprehensive text on the subject—*Dianetics: The Modern Science of Mental Health*.

With the release of *Dianetics* on May 9, 1950, a complete handbook for the application of Ron's new technology was broadly available for the first time. Public interest spread like wildfire. The book shot to the top of the *New York Times* bestseller list and remained there week after week. More than 750 Dianetics study groups sprang up within a few months of its publication.

Ron's work did not stop with the success of *Dianetics* but accelerated, with new discoveries and breakthroughs a constant, normal occurrence. In his further research he discovered the very nature of life itself and its exact relationship to this universe. These discoveries led to his development of Scientology, the first workable technology for the improvement of conditions in any aspect of life.

During his research, Ron explored the subject of radiation, a subject in which he was well grounded from his university days. He conducted intensive studies into the cumulative effects of radiation, as well as those of drugs and other toxic substances, culminating in the development of the Purification program—the first truly workable detoxification program.

Through the 1960s, '70s and into the '80s, Ron continued his research and writing, amassing an enormous volume of material totalling over 60 million words—recorded in books, manuscripts and taped lectures. Today these works are studied and applied daily in hundreds of Scientology churches, missions and organizations around the world.

With his research fully completed and codified, L. Ron Hubbard departed his body on January 24, 1986.

Ron's work opened a wide bridge to understanding and freedom for mankind. Through his efforts, there now exists a totally workable technology with which people can help each other improve their lives and succeed in achieving their goals.

Glossary

Aberration: a departure from rational thought or behavior. It means basically to err, to make mistakes, or more specifically to have fixed ideas which are not true. The word is also used in its scientific sense. It means departure from a straight line. If a line should go from A to B and it is *aberrated*, it would go from A to some other point, to some other point, to some other point, to some other point, to some other point, and finally arrive at B. Taken in its scientific sense, it would also mean the lack of straightness or to see crookedly as, in example, a man sees a horse but thinks he sees an elephant. Aberrated conduct would be wrong conduct, or conduct not supported by reason. Aberration is opposed to sanity, which would be its opposite. From the Latin, *aberrare*, to wander from; Latin, *ab*, away, *errare*, to wander.

acetaldehyde: a colorless, flammable liquid used as a solvent.

adduced: brought forward in argument or as evidence; cited as pertinent or conclusive.

Adenauer: Konrad Adenauer (1876–1967), German statesman; chancellor of the Federal Republic of Germany (West Germany) (1949–63).

Alexander the Great: Alexander III (356–323 B.C.), king of Macedonia, an ancient kingdom located in what is now Greece and Yugoslavia. By conquest, he extended an empire which reached from Greece to India.

amenities: things that add to one's comfort, convenience or pleasure.

"Anderson" type shelter: a small prefabricated air-raid shelter devised by William Paterson, a Scottish engineer, and adopted while Sir John Anderson was the British Home Secretary (1930–40). Anderson shelters were used in Britain during World War II. They were curved, steel huts which some people buried in their gardens and covered with 2 or 3 feet of earth to protect them from the effects of explosion.

annul: to reduce to nothing; obliterate.

antiaircraft: designed for or used in defense against enemy aircraft.

appreciable: sufficient to be readily perceived or estimated; considerable.

arbiter: literally, a person who has the sole or absolute power of judging or determining. Used figuratively in this sense.

arsenic: a silvery white, brittle, very poisonous chemical element, compounds of which are used in making insecticides, glass, medicines, etc.

Assassins: a secret terrorist sect of Muslims of the eleventh to thirteenth century who killed their political enemies as a religious duty. The word "assassin" comes from the Arabic name for this group, "Hashshashin," meaning "addicts of the drug hashish," as hashish was used by the leaders of the group to incite members to assassinate intended victims.

assist: processing which assists the individual to heal himself or be healed by another agency by removing his reasons for precipitating (bringing on) and prolonging his condition and lessening his predisposition (inclination or tendency) to further injure himself or remain in an intolerable condition.

atoll: a ring-shaped coral island nearly or completely surrounding a lagoon.

atom: the smallest component of an element having the chemical properties of that element. It comes from the Greek word *atomos,* undivided.

atomic fission: the splitting of the nucleus of an atom into nuclei of lighter atoms, accompanied by the release of energy. This is the principle of the atomic bomb.

auditing: another word for *processing,* the application of Dianetics or Scientology processes to someone by a trained auditor. *See also* **processing** in this glossary.

auditor: a person trained and qualified in applying Dianetics and/or Scientology processes and procedures to individuals for their betterment; called an auditor because *auditor* means "one who listens."

background radiation: the low radiation from cosmic rays and trace amounts of radioactive substances naturally present in the atmosphere.

barracks: a building or group of buildings for lodging soldiers.

bazooka: a weapon of metal tubing, for aiming and launching electrically fired, armor-piercing rockets.

benzene: a colorless, flammable liquid obtained chiefly from coal tar. It is used for removing grease stains and in making dyes and synthetic rubber. Benzene can cause leukemia and chromosome damage in people exposed to it.

Bikini: an island in the Pacific where atomic bomb tests were conducted in 1946.

binary: designating or of a number system which uses a base of 2 rather than the base of 10 used in the customary number system. The binary system uses combinations of the digits 0 and 1 to express all other numbers.

biochemical: relating to the chemical substances occurring in living organisms.

breeder reactor: a nuclear reactor generating atomic energy and creating additional fuel by producing more fissionable material than it consumes.

bubonic plague: a very dangerous contagious disease, accompanied by fever, chills and swelling of the lymphatic glands. It is carried to humans by fleas from rats or squirrels.

Buck Rogers: the main character of a popular American comic strip, later made into motion pictures. The stories were science fiction, set in the twenty-fifth century.

cadmium: a silver white metallic chemical element found in zinc ores. It is used in some low-melting alloys, electroplating, rechargeable batteries, etc. It has highly toxic dust or fumes.

carbohydrates: organic compounds, such as sugars and starches, composed of carbon, oxygen and hydrogen. Carbohydrates are an important class of foods in animal nutrition, supplying energy to the body.

carbon 14: a radioactive form of carbon which is used as a tracer in chemical and biochemical research. Also, because of its presence in all carbon-containing matter, *carbon 14* provides a means of dating archaeological specimens, fossils, etc., by measuring the amount of radioactive *carbon 14* remaining in them. *See also* **tracer** in this glossary.

carbon tetrachloride: a colorless, nonflammable liquid, often used in fire extinguishers and in cleaning fluids. Its fumes are very dangerous if inhaled.

case: a person's mental condition. A person's *case* is the way he responds to the world around him by reason of his aberrations.

catalyze: to cause or accelerate a chemical change without the substance causing the change being affected.

cataracts: areas in the lens of the eye which have become opaque due to disease, causing partial or total blindness.

cavalrymen: soldiers in the part of a military force composed of troops that serve on horseback.

Chernobyl: a city in the USSR, site of a nuclear reactor plant where, in late April 1986, systems malfunctioned causing an explosion of one of the reactor buildings and a fire of a reactor core. Radiation contamination from this accident spread across much of the western USSR as well as eastern and central Europe and Scandinavia.

chlordane: a highly poisonous, volatile oil, formerly used as an insecticide.

chromosome: any of the microscopic rod-shaped bodies in a cell that carry the genes that convey hereditary characteristics.

chronicled: recorded as a chronological record of events or history.

citadel: any strong fortified place; stronghold.

claustrophobia: an abnormal fear of being in enclosed or narrow places.

close terminals with: to collapse into or identify oneself with something. *See also* **closure of terminals** and **terminal** in this glossary.

closure of terminals: the phenomenon of terminals (people, fixed masses, etc.) collapsing into each other or becoming identified, one with the other. *See also* **terminal** in this glossary.

cobalt 60: a radioactive form of cobalt, a hard, lustrous steel gray metallic element.

cocaine: a bitter, crystalline drug obtained from the dried leaves of the coca shrub; it is a local anesthetic and a dangerous, illegal stimulant.

colitis: inflammation of the large intestine.

combusting: burning.

congenital: of or pertaining to a condition present at birth, whether inherited or caused by the environment, especially the uterine environment.

constituent: an element of which something is composed or made up; component.

control rod: a neutron-absorbing material in the shape of a rod or other arrangement of parts, that can be moved into or out of the core of a nuclear reactor to regulate the rate of fission.

cosmic rays: radiations of high penetrating power that originate in outer space and consist partly of high-energy atomic nuclei.

curie: a unit of measurement of radiation. The *curie* is a representation of how fast a piece of radioactive material disintegrates. Radioactivity is generated by the disintegration of the atoms in an unstable element. One *curie* of radioactivity is defined as 37 billion disintegrations per second. The *curie* measures the amount of radioactive material from the viewpoint of how much action is going on in it. There are also other ways of measuring the amount of radiation or the amount of effect radiation has on a given substance.

Darwin, Charles Robert: (1809–1882) English naturalist and author; originated theory of evolution by natural selection. *See also* **natural selection** in this glossary.

debility: weakness or feebleness, especially of the body.

decontamination: the action of making (an object or area) safe for unprotected personnel by removing, neutralizing, or destroying any harmful substance, as radioactive material or poisonous gas.

deleterious: harmful, injurious.

desensitizes: becomes less sensitive; becomes less affected or likely to be affected by a specified stimulus.

detoxified: changed (toxins) into less toxic or more readily excretable substances.

diabolical: having the qualities of a devil; fiendish; outrageously wicked.

Dianazene: a formula combining nicotinic acid with other vitamins and minerals which was developed to make the intake of nicotinic acid more effective in handling radiation.

Dianetics: Dianetics spiritual healing technology. It addresses and handles the effects of the spirit on the body and can alleviate such things as unwanted sensations and emotions, accidents, injuries and psychosomatic illnesses (ones that are caused or aggravated by mental stress). *Dianetics* means "through the soul" (from Greek *dia,* through, and *nous,* soul). It is further defined as "what the soul is doing to the body."

dicalcium phosphate: a substance consisting of calcium and phosphorus used as a mineral supplement in the Dianazene formula.

effect: a point of receipt of flow (thought, energy or action). For example: If one considers a river flowing to the sea, the place where it began would be the source-point or cause, the place where it went into the sea would be the effect-point, and the sea would be the effect of the river. A man firing a gun is cause; a man receiving a bullet is effect.

Einstein, Albert: (1879–1955), German physicist, US citizen from 1940; formulated the theory of the conversion of mass into energy, opening the way for the development of the atomic bomb.

electrodes: conductors through which an electric current enters or leaves a nonmetallic medium.

electron: a negatively charged particle that forms a part of all atoms, and can exist on its own in a free state.

element: any substance that cannot be separated into different substances by ordinary chemical methods; all matter is composed of such substances. Elements can be transformed into other elements by radioactive decay or by nuclear reactions.

E-Meter: an electronic device for measuring the mental state or change of state of *Homo sapiens.* It is *not* a lie detector. It does not diagnose or cure anything. It is used by auditors to assist people in locating areas of spiritual distress or travail.

enzymes: complex organic substances secreted by certain cells of plants and animals which cause a chemical change in the substance upon which they act.

equilibrium: mental or emotional balance; evenness of mind or temper; composure.

exudation: the action of coming out gradually in drops, as sweat, through pores or small openings; oozing out.

fallout: the descent to earth of radioactive particles, as after a nuclear explosion or reactor accident; also the radioactive particles themselves.

feather their own nests: obtain money, ethically or unethically, for themselves; obtain money or an unfair share of money from the efforts of others; provide for oneself with no regard to the welfare of others.

ferrous gluconate: a type of iron supplement compound, containing considerably more absorbable iron than other types.

fictitiously: of, pertaining to or consisting of fiction; imaginatively produced or set forth; created by the imagination.

fission: the act of cleaving or splitting into parts. Nuclear *fission* is the splitting of the nucleus of an atom into nuclei of lighter atoms, accompanied by the release of energy. The word comes from Latin *fission*, meaning "a splitting, dividing."

fissionable: capable of or possessing a nucleus or nuclei capable of undergoing fission. *See also* **fission** in this glossary.

formaldehyde: a colorless, toxic gas, having a suffocating odor; used chiefly as a disinfectant and preservative. It has been linked to forms of cancer and is toxic to the central nervous system.

Four Horsemen: Four Horsemen of the Apocalypse: four riders on white, red, black and pale horses, symbolizing the pestilence, war, famine and death which are prophesied in the Apocalypse, or book of Revelation, the last book of the New Testament in the Bible.

fuel rod: nuclear fuel contained in a long thin-walled tube, an array of such tubes forming the core of a nuclear reactor.

fusion: the combining of lightweight atomic nuclei into a nucleus of heavier mass with the release of great amounts of energy, as in a hydrogen bomb.

gamma rays: radiations which are similar to X-rays, but with a shorter wavelength than X-rays. Because of their short wavelength, gamma rays are very penetrating. They have a range in air of about 1½ miles and are the principal cause of radiation disease in atomic warfare.

gastroenteritis: an inflammation of the stomach and the intestines.

Geiger counter: an instrument used for detecting and measuring radioactivity; named after H. Geiger (1882–1945), German physicist.

genes: any of the units occurring at specific points on the chromosomes by which specific hereditary characters are passed on to the next generation.

geneticist: a specialist or expert in genetics, the science of heredity, dealing with resemblances and differences of related organisms resulting from the interaction of their genes and the environment.

Genghis Khan: (1162–1227) Mongol conqueror of most of Asia and of East Europe. He was known to be ruthless in war, but he built an empire which lasted until 1368.

glibly: done in a smooth, offhand fashion.

gonads: organs in which reproductive cells develop in the male or female; sex glands. Ovaries and testicles are gonads.

granite: a hard, coarse-grained rock, much used for buildings and monuments.

granting beingness: the ability or willingness to let someone else be what he is. *Beingness* is defined as the assumption of a category of identity. An example of beingness would be one's own name. Another example would be one's profession. Another example would be one's physical characteristics. Each or all of these things could be called one's beingness. Beingness is assumed by oneself or given to oneself, or is attained. For example, in the playing of a game each player has his own beingness. Listening to what someone has to say and taking care to understand them, being courteous, refraining from needless criticism, expressing admiration or affinity are examples of the actions of someone who can grant others beingness. The ability to grant others beingness is one of the highest virtues one can have.

group auditing: Scientology auditing techniques administered to groups of children or adults.

hand in glove: very intimately associated.

hashish: a drug made from the resin contained in the flowering tops of hemp, chewed or smoked for its intoxicating and euphoric effects.

heptachlor: a waxy solid, formerly used as an insecticide.

hereditary: passing, or capable of passing, naturally from parent to offspring through the genes.

Hiroshima: a seaport in southwest Japan; site of the first military use of the atomic bomb on 6 August 1945.

hives: a disease in which the skin itches and shows raised, white welts, caused by a sensitivity to certain foods or a reaction to heat, light, etc.

Homer: semilegendary Greek poet of circa eighth century B.C.: The *Iliad* and the *Odyssey* are both attributed to him.

houris: beautiful virgins provided in Paradise for all faithful Muslims.

hydrogen bomb: a bomb, more powerful than an atomic bomb, that derives its explosive energy from the thermonuclear fusion reaction of certain forms of hydrogen. *See also* **thermonuclear** in this glossary.

impregnated: infused or permeated throughout, as with a substance; saturated.

incandescent: glowing or white with heat.

incursions: hostile entrances into or invasions of a place or territory, especially sudden ones; raids.

infantry: soldiers or military units that fight on foot, in modern times typically with rifles, machine guns, grenades, etc., as weapons.

infirm: feeble or weak in body and in health, especially because of age; ailing.

inverse square law: (*physics, optics*) one of several laws relating two quantities such that one quantity varies inversely as the square of the other. There are laws using this basic principle which apply to magnetism, sound and light. An example of this would be that of the illumination produced on a screen by a point source of light: if the distance between the light source and screen were doubled, the illumination on the screen would be reduced to a quarter of its original intensity; if the distance were trebled, the illumination would be reduced to one-ninth; if the distance were quadrupled, the illumination would be reduced to one-sixteenth, etc. Likewise, the intensity of sound decreases as the distance from its source increases: a bell 10 feet away sounds one-fourth as loud as the same bell 5 feet away; and if 15 feet away, it sounds one-ninth as loud as when 5 feet away. Applied to radiation, the *inverse square law* states that the intensity of radiation decreases in proportion to the square of the distance from its source.

invested: surrounded with military forces so as to prevent approach or escape; besieged.

iodine 131: a radioactive form of iodine, used especially in the diagnosis and treatment of thyroid function, in internal radiation therapy and as a tracer. *See also* **tracer** in this glossary.

irradiation: exposure or the process of exposure to X-rays or other radiation.

Ismailian Shiites: a fanatical sect of Muslims who are in disagreement with many of the accepted doctrines of the main group of Muslim believers.

Kaiser Bill: William II (1859–1941), emperor of Germany (1888–1918). (*Kaiser* is German for "emperor.") Through inept handling of his power and authority as emperor, he helped cause the circumstances leading to World War I and thereby the deaths of millions of men on the battlefields.

kiloton: an explosive force equal to that of 1,000 tons of TNT. *See also* **TNT** in this glossary.

Kremlin: the chief office of the government of the Soviet Union, in Moscow.

LD: abbreviation for lethal dose.

leukemia: any of several cancers of the bone marrow that prevent the normal manufacture of red and white blood cells and platelets (the minute bodies in the blood that aid in coagulation), resulting in anemia, increased susceptibility to infection and impaired blood clotting.

liberated: disengaged; set free from combination.

lymphatic tissue: tissue in the body which creates or conveys *lymph,* a clear, yellowish fluid containing white blood cells in a liquid resembling blood plasma.

man-of-war: an armed naval vessel; warship.

marijuana: the dried leaves and flowers of the hemp plant, used in cigarette form as a narcotic or hallucinogen.

megaton: the explosive force of a million tons of TNT. A 15-megaton bomb is the equivalent of 15 million tons of TNT.

meltdown: a situation in which a rapid rise in the power level of a nuclear reactor, as from a defect in the cooling system, results in the melting of the fuel rods and the release of dangerous radiation and may cause the core to sink into the earth.

mercury: a heavy, silver white metallic element that is liquid at ordinary temperatures; quicksilver. Ingestion of mercury (for example, by eating fish caught in polluted waters) can damage the central nervous system, causing tremors and poor coordination and, in severe cases, brain damage.

Mindszenty: Jozsef Mindszenty (1892–1975), Hungarian primate (highest ranking bishop in the country) and Roman Catholic cardinal. An opponent of communism, he was arrested by the Hungarian government in 1948.

ministrations: acts or instances of giving help or care; service, especially in religious matters.

molecule: the smallest particle of an element or compound that can exist in the free state and still retain the characteristics of the element or compound: The molecules of elements consist of one atom or two or more similar atoms; those of compounds consist of two or more different atoms.

Nagasaki: a seaport in southwest Japan; site of the second military use of the atomic bomb on 9 August 1945.

natural selection: a process in nature resulting in the survival and perpetuation of only those forms of plant and animal life having certain favorable characteristics that best enable them to adapt to a specific environment.

neutron: one of the particles that make up the nucleus of an atom. A neutron has no electrical charge.

niacin: a white, odorless, crystalline substance found in protein foods or prepared synthetically. It is a member of the vitamin B complex. *See also* **vitamin B complex** in this glossary.

niacinamide: a form of niacin invented by the medical profession to avoid the flush which is turned on when a person takes niacin. What the medical profession didn't realize was that niacin itself doesn't turn on a flush—the flush is caused by the fact that sunburn or radiation is being run out. Niacinamide is worthless for the purpose of running out radiation.

nickel: a hard, silvery white metallic element, much used as an alloy and in electroplating. Certain forms of nickel are toxic when inhaled into the body as dust.

nicotinic acid: same as **niacin**. *See* **niacin** in this glossary.

nitrogen dioxide: a highly toxic brownish gas, used as an industrial chemical and also released as an air pollutant during the burning of fossil fuels such as coal, oil or natural gas.

no-game condition: a condition in which no game is possible, defining *game* as a contest of person against person or team against team. A game consists of freedoms, barriers and purposes. There is freedom among barriers. If the barriers are known and the freedoms are known, there can be a game. A no-game condition would therefore be a totality of barriers or a totality of freedom.

North African campaigns: a series of battles between Germany and Great Britain during World War II, fought in the desert of North Africa.

nuclear: of, characterized by, or operated by the use of atomic energy.

nuclear physics: that branch of physics (the science of relationships between matter and energy) which deals with atoms, their nuclear structure, and the behavior of nuclear particles.

nuclear reactor: an apparatus in which an atomic fission chain reaction can be initiated, sustained and controlled, for generating heat or producing useful radiation.

nuclei: plural of **nucleus**. *See* **nucleus** in this glossary.

nucleus: the central part of an atom, composed of protons and neutrons and making up almost all of the mass of the atom: It carries a positive charge.

Old Man of the Mountain: another name for al-Hasan ibn-al-Sabbah (died 1124), founder of the sect of Assassins.

onus: difficult obligation, task, burden, etc.

orifices: openings or apertures which serve as or have the form of a mouth, as of a tube, of the stomach, bladder or other bodily organ, of a wound, etc.; the mouth of any cavity.

ovaries: female reproductive glands producing eggs and, in vertebrates, sex hormones.

overt act: an act by the person or individual leading to the injury, reduction or degradation of another, others or their persons, possessions or associations. It can be intentional or unintentional.

ozone: a form of oxygen with a sharp odor, produced by electricity and present in the air, especially after a thunderstorm. It is also one of the toxic pollutants present in smog.

Pavlov, Ivan Petrovich: (1849–1936), Russian physiologist; noted for behavioral experiments on dogs.

pharmacopeia: an authoritative book containing a list and description of drugs and medicinal products together with the standards established under law for their production, dispensation, use, etc.

photons: units of energy having both particle and wave behavior: they have no charge or mass but possess momentum. The energy of light, X-rays, gamma rays, etc., is carried by photons.

piecework: work done and paid for by the piece.

placenta: an organ that develops in the womb during pregnancy and supplies the fetus with nourishment.

plutonium: a radioactive chemical element, used in nuclear weapons and reactors.

postulates: conclusions, decisions or resolutions made by the individual himself to resolve a problem or set a pattern for the future or nullify a pattern of the past.

prank: a trick of an amusing, playful or sometimes malicious nature.

present time: the time which is now and which becomes the past almost as rapidly as it is observed. It is a term loosely applied to the environment existing in now.

Problems of Work, The: a book by L. Ron Hubbard on the subject of work. This contains solutions to the basic difficulties associated with work, such as overcoming exhaustion, the secrets of efficiency, handling confusing situations and much more.

process: a set of questions asked or commands given by an auditor to help a person find out things about himself or life and to improve his condition.

processing: the application of Dianetics or Scientology processes to someone by a trained auditor. The exact definition of processing is: The action of asking a person a question (which he can understand and answer), getting an answer to that question and acknowledging him for that answer. Also called **auditing.**

propaganda: information, ideas or rumors deliberately widely spread to help or harm a person, group, movement, institution, nation, etc.

propagandists: people involved in producing or spreading propaganda. *See also* **propaganda** in this glossary.

proton: one of the particles that make up the nucleus of an atom. A *proton* has a single positive electric charge.

provocateurs: people who provoke trouble, cause dissension or the like; agitators.

psychopath: a person whose behavior is largely amoral and asocial and who is characterized by irresponsibility, lack of remorse or shame, perverse or impulsive (often criminal) behavior and other serious personality defects, generally without psychotic attacks or symptoms.

puerperal fever: a poisoned state of the birth canal and the bloodstream occurring at childbirth. Also called childbed fever.

radiation sickness: sickness caused by irradiation with X-rays or other nuclear radiation as a result of therapeutic treatment, accidental exposure, or a nuclear bomb explosion and characterized by nausea, vomiting, headache, cramps, diarrhea, loss of hair and teeth, destruction of white blood cells, and prolonged hemorrhage.

radioactive: giving off, or capable of giving off, radiant energy in the form of particles or rays by the spontaneous disintegration of atomic nuclei: said of certain elements, as plutonium, uranium, etc., and their products.

radiologists: those who deal with X-rays or nuclear radiation, especially for medical uses.

radiotherapy: treatment of diseases by means of X-rays or of radioactive substances.

reactor: *See* **nuclear reactor** in this glossary.

restimulation: reactivation of a past memory due to similar circumstances in the present approximating circumstances of the past.

Robespierres: persons similar to Maximilien Robespierre (1758–94), one of the leaders of the French Revolution whose name is closely associated with the 2,500 people who were guillotined during the Revolution.

roentgen: (*physics*) the unit of exposure to X-rays or gamma rays. Whereas a *curie* measures the amount of activity in radioactive material itself, a *roentgen* is a measure of the radiation generated by that material. Named after German physicist Wilhelm Conrad Röntgen (1845–1923) who discovered X-rays in 1895. Abbreviation *r*.

runs out: erases, causes to disappear.

saber-rattling: a show or threat of military power, especially as used by a nation to impose its policies on other countries.

saboteurs: people who engage in deliberate obstruction of or damage to any cause, movement, activity, effort, etc.

scimitar: a curved, single-edged sword of Oriental origin.

Scientology: Scientology philosophy. It is the study and handling of the spirit in relationship to itself, universes and other life. Scientology means *scio*, knowing in the fullest sense of the word and *logos*, study. In itself the word means literally *knowing how to know*. Scientology is a "route," a way, rather than a dissertation or an assertive body of knowledge. Through its drills and studies one may find the truth for himself. The technology is therefore not expounded as something to believe, but something to *do*.

sentry: a soldier stationed at a place to stand guard and prevent the passage of unauthorized persons, watch for fires, etc., especially a sentinel stationed at a pass, gate, opening in a defense work, or the like.

sinusitis: inflammation of one or more sinuses in the skull. (*Sinuses* are the cavities in the skull connecting with the nostrils).

smallpox: an acute, highly contagious virus disease characterized by prolonged fever, vomiting, and pustular (of a swelling filled with pus) eruptions that often leave pitted scars, or pockmarks, when healed.

sovereign: having supreme and independent power or authority in government, as possessed or claimed by a state or community.

Stalin: Joseph Stalin (1879-1953), Russian political leader. As general secretary of the Communist Party, he expelled those who opposed him and ordered the arrest and deportation to Siberia and northern Russia of tens of thousands of members of the opposition. He became premier of the Soviet Union in 1941, and established himself as virtual dictator.

standing electrical wave: an electrical wave which, instead of traveling from one point to another, is stationary. This is due to interactions between a wave transmitted down a line and a wave reflected back. If you can imagine an ocean wave which was no longer rolling but was just sitting there peaked, that would be an example of a standing wave. As another example, a vibrating rope tied at one end will produce a standing wave (see figure below).

1. Wave traveling in one direction.

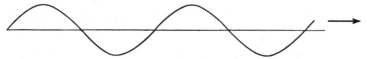

2. Wave traveling in opposite direction.

3. The above two waves produce a standing wave.

steppes: vast, treeless plains.

strontium 90: a radioactive form of the element strontium (a pale yellow metallic chemical element), present in fallout from nuclear explosions. Strontium 90 can be absorbed into the bones in place of calcium, hindering further absorption of calcium and leading to weak bones.

subatomic: of or pertaining to the inner part of an atom or to a particle smaller than an atom.

sulfur dioxide: a colorless, nonflammable, suffocating gas, formed when sulfur burns; used chiefly in the manufacture of chemicals such as sulfuric acid, in preserving fruits and vegetables, and in bleaching, disinfecting and fumigating.

terminal: something that has mass and meaning; a point from which energy can flow or by which energy can be received.

Tesla, Nikola: (1856–1943), US physicist, electrical engineer and inventor, born in Austria-Hungary. Among his inventions were generators of high-frequency currents and wireless systems of communication and of power transmission.

testes: the male reproductive glands, two oval glands located in the scrotum.

therapeutics: the branch of medicine that deals with the treatment and cure of diseases; therapy.

thermonuclear: of, pertaining to or involving the nuclear fusion reaction that takes place between the nuclei of a gas, especially hydrogen, heated to a temperature of several million degrees.

thinkingness: potential of considering; the combination of past observations to derive a future observation.

Three Mile Island: the location of a reactor facility outside Harrisburg, Pennsylvania, where in March, 1979 a series of human and equipment failures caused a significant meltdown of nuclear fuel and the escape of a cloud of radioactive gas.

TNT: a high explosive unaffected by ordinary friction or shock: used chiefly in military and other explosive devices. *TNT* is short for *trinitrotoluene.*

toluene: a colorless, flammable, aromatic liquid obtained from coal tar and petroleum and used as a solvent and for making explosives, dyes, etc.

tower musket: a firearm of the sixteenth century. It was very long and heavy and had to be rested on a post on the ground for support when in use.

toxic: acting as or having the effect of a poison, poisonous.

tracer: a substance, especially a radioactive one, used to follow a chemical process or a complex sequence of biochemical reactions (as in an animal body), to locate diseased cells and tissues, to determine physical properties, etc.

Trafalgar Square: one of the main public squares in London, named after the battle of Trafalgar, in which Lord Horatio

Nelson's British fleet overwhelmingly defeated a large fleet of French and Spanish ships. Trafalgar Square has in it a 168-foot-tall monument to Lord Nelson.

tramp steamer: a freight vessel that does not run regularly between fixed ports, but takes a cargo wherever shippers desire.

Troy: ancient ruined city in Asia Minor, site of the Trojan War—a ten-year war waged against Troy by the Greeks to recover a Greek king's wife, Helen, who had been abducted by Paris, a Trojan.

tumultuous: full of tumult or riotousness; marked by disturbance and uproar.

turn on: start suddenly to affect or show.

ultraviolet: pertaining to a band of radiation having wavelengths that are shorter than violet light.

unfissioned plutonium: small particles of plutonium which have not undergone fission in a nuclear reaction. *See also* **plutonium** and **fission** in this glossary.

United Nations: an international organization with headquarters in New York City, formed to promote international peace, security, and cooperation under the terms of the charter signed by fifty-one founding countries in San Francisco in 1945.

uptake: absorption.

uranium: a very hard, heavy, silvery radioactive metallic chemical element: It is found only in combination, chiefly in pitchblende (a brown to black lustrous mineral), and is important in work on atomic energy.

vitamin A: a vitamin important in bone growth, healthy skin, sexual function and reproduction.

vitamin B$_1$: a vitamin, also called thiamine, important to the body in the functions of cell oxidation (respiration), growth, carbohydrate metabolism, stimulation and transmission of nerve impulses, etc.

vitamin B$_2$: also called riboflavin, a vitamin important in the metabolism of protein and in skin, liver and eye health.

vitamin B complex: an important group of water-soluble vitamins found in liver, yeast, etc., including vitamin B_1, vitamin B_2 and niacin.

vitamin C: also called ascorbic acid; a colorless, crystalline, water-soluble vitamin, found in many foods, especially citrus fruits, vegetables and rose hips and also made synthetically; it is required for proper nutrition and metabolism.

vitamin D: a vitamin which is important in bone health and growth, calcium metabolism, nerve health and regulation of heartbeat.

vitamin E: a vitamin important in keeping oxygen from combining with waste products to form toxic compounds, and in red blood cell health.

vogue: something in fashion, as at a particular time.

vying: competing; contending.

wavelength: the distance from any point in a wave, as of light or sound, to the same point in the next wave of the series.

Western Electric: an American electrical company.

whooping cough: an infectious bacterial disease usually of children, characterized by inflammation of the air passages, with convulsive fits of coughing that end with a loud, gasping sound (whoop).

Windscale: the name and location of a nuclear plant (now called Sellafield) in England, 300 miles northwest of London, where in 1957 a uranium fuel element burst, causing a uranium fire and a major release of radiation into the atmosphere. Fallout from the accident was measured in Ireland, London, Mol (Belgium) and Frankfurt.

Wundt, Wilhelm: (1832–1920) German physiologist and psychologist; the originator of the false doctrine that man is no more than an animal.

X-rays: a form of radiation similar to light but of a shorter wavelength and capable of penetrating solids; used in medicine for study, diagnosis and treatment of certain organic disorders, especially of internal structures of the body.

Index

Where to Do the Purification Program

For information on where to do the Purification program, contact the nearest Scientology church or organization listed at the back of this book.

Churches of Scientology have been delivering the Purification program as part of its spiritual counseling procedures since its release in 1979.

Books and Tapes
by L. Ron Hubbard

Purification Book Package

The books in the Purification Book Package (which includes *All About Radiation*) contain data on the only effective way of handling drug and toxic residuals in the body, clearing the way for real mental and spiritual improvement—the Purification program. These books are available individually and as a specially boxed set.

Clear Body, Clear Mind: The Effective Purification Program • This book contains all the information on L. Ron Hubbard's Purification program. This is the only program of its kind in existence that has been found to clean the residues of drugs, toxins and elements harmful to human bodies out of them! Drugs and chemicals can stop a person's ability to improve himself or just to live life. This book describes the program which can make it possible to start living again.

Purification: An Illustrated Answer to Drugs • Presented in a concise, fully illustrated format, this book provides you with an overview of the Purification program. Our society is ridden by abuse of drugs, alcohol and medicine that reduce one's ability to think clearly. This book lays out what can be done about it, in a form which is easy for anyone to read and understand.

Purification Rundown Delivery Manual • This book is a manual which guides a person through the Purification Rundown step by step. It includes all of the needed reports as well as spaces for the person to write his successes and to attest to program completion. This manual makes administering the Purification Rundown simple and *standard*.

Basic Scientology Books

The Basic Scientology Books Package contains the knowledge you need to be able to improve conditions in life. These books are available individually or as a set, complete with an attractive slipcase.

Scientology: The Fundamentals of Thought • Improve life *and* make a better world with this easy-to-read book that lays out the fundamental truths about life and thought. No such knowledge has ever before existed, and no such results have ever before been attainable as those which can be reached by the use of this knowledge. Equipped with this book alone, one could perform seeming miracles in changing the states of health, ability and intelligence of people. This *is* how life works. This *is* how you change men, women and children for the better, and attain greater personal freedom.

A New Slant on Life • Have you ever asked yourself, Who am I? What am I? This book of articles by L. Ron Hubbard answers these all-too-common questions. This is knowledge one can use every day—for a new, more confident and happier slant on life!

The Problems of Work • Work plays a big part in the game of life. Do you really enjoy your work? Are you certain of your job security? Would you like the increased personal satisfaction of doing your work well? This is the book that shows exactly how to achieve these things and more. The game of life—and within it, the game of work—can be enjoyable and rewarding.

Scientology 0-8: The Book of Basics • What is life? Did you know an individual can create space, energy and time? Here are the basics of life itself, and the secrets of becoming cause over any area of your life. Discover how you can use the data in this book to achieve your goals.

Basic Dictionary of Dianetics and Scientology • Compiled from the works of L. Ron Hubbard, this convenient dictionary contains the terms and expressions needed by anyone learning Dianetics and Scientology technology. And a *special bonus*—an easy-to-read Scientology organizing board chart that shows you who to contact for services and information at your nearest Scientology organization.

Basic Dianetics Books

The Basic Dianetics Books Package is your complete guide to the inner workings of the mind. You can get all of these books individually or in a set, complete with an attractive slipcase.

Dianetics: The Modern Science of Mental Health • Acclaimed as the most effective self-help book ever published. Dianetics technology has helped millions reach new heights of freedom and ability. Millions of copies are sold every year! Discover the source of mental barriers that prevent you from achieving your goals—and how to handle them!

The Dynamics of Life • Break through the barriers to your happiness. This is the first book Ron wrote detailing the startling principles behind Dianetics—facts so powerful they can change forever the way you look at yourself and your potentials. Discover how you can use the powerful basic principles in this book to blast through the barriers of your mind and gain full control over your success, future and happiness.

Self Analysis • The complete do-it-yourself handbook for anyone who wants to improve their abilities and success potential.

Use the simple, easy-to-learn techniques in *Self Analysis* to build self-confidence and reduce stress.

Dianetics: The Evolution of a Science • It is estimated that we use less than ten percent of our mind's potential. What stops us from developing and using the full potential of our minds? *Dianetics: The Evolution of a Science* is L. Ron Hubbard's incredible story of how he discovered the reactive mind and how he developed the keys to unlock its secrets. Get this firsthand account of what the mind really is, and how you can release its hidden potential.

Dianetics Graduate Books

These books by L. Ron Hubbard give you detailed knowledge of how the mind works—data you can use to help yourself and others break out of the traps of life. While you can get these books individually, the Dianetics Graduate Books Package can also be purchased as a set, complete with an attractive slipcase.

Science of Survival • If you ever wondered why people act the way they do, you'll find this book a wealth of information. It's vital to anyone who wants to understand others and improve personal relationships. *Science of Survival* is built around a remarkable chart—The Hubbard Chart of Human Evaluation. With it you can understand and predict other people's behavior and reactions and greatly increase your control over your own life. This is a valuable handbook that can make a difference between success and failure on the job and in life.

Dianetics 55! • Your success in life depends on your ability to communicate. Do you know a formula exists for communication? Learn the rules of better communication that can help you live a more fulfilling life. Here, L. Ron Hubbard deals with the fundamental principles of communication and how you can master these to achieve your goals.

Advanced Procedure and Axioms • For the *first* time the basics of thought and the physical universe have been codified into a set of fundamental laws, signaling an entirely new way to view and approach the subjects of man, the physical universe and even life itself.

Handbook for Preclears • Written as an advanced personal workbook, *Handbook for Preclears* contains easily done processes to help you overcome the effect of times you were not in control of your life, times that your emotions were a barrier to your success and much more. Completing all the fifteen auditing steps contained in this book sets you up for really being in *control* of your environment and life.

Child Dianetics • Here is a revolutionary new approach to rearing children with Dianetics auditing techniques. Find out how you can help your child achieve greater confidence, more self-reliance, improved learning rate and a happier, more loving relationship with you.

Notes on the Lectures of L. Ron Hubbard • Compiled from his fascinating lectures given shortly after the publication of *Dianetics: The Modern Science of Mental Health*, this book contains some of the first material Ron ever released on the ARC triangle and the Tone Scale, and how these discoveries relate to auditing.

OT[1] Library Package

All the following books contain the knowledge of a spiritual being's relationship to this universe and how his abilities

---

1. **OT:** abbreviation for *Operating Thetan,* a state of beingness. It is a being "at cause over matter, energy, space, time, form and life." *Operating* comes from "able to operate without dependency on things," and *thetan* is the Greek letter *theta* (θ), which the Greeks used to represent *thought* or perhaps *spirit,* to which an *n* is added to make a noun in the modern style used to create words in engineering. It is also θ^n or "theta to the nth degree," meaning unlimited or vast.

---

to operate successfully in it can be restored. You can get all of these books individually or in a set, complete with an attractive slipcase.

Scientology 8-80 • What are the laws of life? We are all familiar with physical laws such as the law of gravity, but what laws govern life and thought? L. Ron Hubbard answers the riddles of life and its goals in the physical universe.

Scientology 8-8008 • Get the basic truths about your nature as a spiritual being and your relationship to the physical universe around you. Here, L. Ron Hubbard describes procedures designed to increase your abilities to heights previously only dreamed of.

Scientology: A History of Man • A fascinating look at the evolutionary background and history of the human race. This was Ron's first book on the vast time track of man. As Ron said, "This is a cold-blooded and factual account of your last sixty trillion years."

The Creation of Human Ability • This book contains processes designed to restore the power of a thetan over his own postulates, to understand the nature of his beingness, to free his self-determinism and much, much more.

Basic Executive Books

The Basic Executive Books Package consists of the book *The Problems of Work* and the two books listed below. They are available individually or as a set, complete with an attractive slipcase.

How to Live Though an Executive • What are the factors in business and commerce which, if lacking, can keep a person overworked and worried, keep labor and management at each other's throats, and make an unsafe working atmosphere? L. Ron Hubbard reveals principles based on years of research into many different types of organizations.

Introduction to Scientology Ethics • A complete knowledge of ethics is vital to anyone's success in life. Without knowing and applying the information in this book, success is only a matter of luck or chance. That is not much to look forward to. This book contains the answers to questions like, "How do I know when a decision is right or wrong?" "How can I predictably improve things around me?" The powerful ethics technology of L. Ron Hubbard is your way to ever-increasing survival.

The E-Meter Books Package

The following books on the E-Meter give all the data you need to understand and professionally operate your E-Meter. You can get all of these books individually or in a set, with an attractive slipcase.

Introducing the E-Meter • This is a basic book that introduces you to the E-Meter spiritual counseling device and its operation.

Understanding the E-Meter • A large, illustrated book that fully explains the basics of the E-Meter device, how it works and how it can measure the electrical activity of thought. Any question on the principles of the E-Meter can be answered with this book.

E-Meter Essentials • This book gives more advanced aspects of E-Meter use, plus a detailed description of the different types of reads on the meter and what they mean.

The Book of E-Meter Drills • With this book you learn all phases of E-Meter operation with detailed, hands-on drills.

Other Scientology Books

What Is Scientology? • Scientology works. It covers every aspect of life and livingness. But how do you communicate it to someone who has not yet experienced it for himself?

The answer is simple—the all-new edition of *What Is Scientology?*

The most comprehensive text ever assembled on the Scientology religion, this book covers its religious heritage, basic principles and practices, organizational structure, worldwide use and expansion, social betterment programs and much, much more.

What Is Scientology? is *the* definitive reference for anyone who wants *all* the facts on the world's fastest growing religion.

Understanding: The Universal Solvent • L. Ron Hubbard's works contain a wisdom which is extraordinary in its perception and power. *Understanding: The Universal Solvent* is a collection of quotations from those works containing over 450 quotes, fully categorized and indexed for ease of reading. This book covers, in concise, strikingly beautiful and often poetic form, some of the most basic truths in this universe.

Knowingness • This collection of quotations has been designed especially for the Scientologist. It contains passages assembled from a broad selection of L. Ron Hubbard's writings and recorded lectures, imparting powerful and poetic truths about ability, mankind and life.

Art • The full collection of L. Ron Hubbard's writings on art, this book cuts through the fog of conflicting opinions on the subject and establishes fundamentals that are vital to any artistic endeavor. Beginning with a simple, workable definition of what art really is and including an analysis of what makes a work of art *good* as opposed to mediocre or poor, the chapters of this book contain basic principles that you can apply—in your art, in your profession and in life itself.

Have You Lived Before This Life? • This is the book that sparked a flood of interest in the ancient puzzle: Does man live only one life? The answer lay in mystery, buried until L. Ron Hubbard's researches unearthed the truth. Actual case histories of people recalling past lives in auditing tell the tale.

Dianetics and Scientology Technical Dictionary • This dictionary is your indispensable guide to the words and ideas of Scientology and Dianetics technologies—technologies which can help you increase your know-how and effectiveness in life. Over three thousand words are defined—including a new understanding of vital words like *life, love* and *happiness* as well as Scientology terms.

Modern Management Technology Defined: Hubbard Dictionary of Administration and Management • Here's a real breakthrough in the subject of administration and management! Eighty-six hundred words are defined for greater understanding of any business situation. Clear, precise Scientology definitions describe many previously baffling phenomena and bring truth, sanity and understanding to the often murky field of business management.

Organization Executive Course • The *Organization Executive Course* volumes contain organizational technology never before known to man. This is not just how a Scientology organization works; this is how the operation of *any* organization, *any* activity, can be improved. A person knowing the data in these volumes fully, and applying it, could completely reverse any downtrend in a company—or even a country!

Management Series Volumes 1, 2 and 3 • These books contain technology that anyone who works with management in any way must know completely to be a true success. Contained in these books are such subjects as data evaluation, the technology of how to organize any area for maximum production and expansion, how to handle personnel, the actual technology of public relations and much more.

Ceremonies of the Church of Scientology • Discover the beautiful and inspiring ceremonies of the Church of Scientology. This book contains the illuminating Creed of the Church, church services, sermons and ceremonies.

Introductory and Demonstration Processes Handbook • What's the best way to give someone reality on Scientology and what it can do? *Audit* him! This extensive, easy-to-use handbook equips you with a complete array of introductory and demonstration processes that you can use anywhere—on a bus, in a cafe, at the shopping mall or at home with family and friends.

Assists Processing Handbook • Have you ever wished you could really help a person who was ill, injured or in pain? This book shows you how. A full collection of assist processes used in Dianetics and Scientology, this handbook includes assists developed by L. Ron Hubbard to help ease arthritis, make a person sober, bring down someone's temperature, aid a pregnant woman or a child, and even to help relieve the common cold.

Group Auditor's Handbook • Is it possible to improve the alertness, awareness and communication of a whole group of people, all at one time? Yes—using Group Processing. The *Group Auditor's Handbook* contains the fundamentals of this powerful technology, all the details of how to set up and run a Group Processing session, *and* the auditing commands for thirty-two different Group Auditing sessions. Group Processing is a skill any Scientologist can learn and apply to improve society on a broad scale.

Volunteer Minister's Handbook • This is a big, practical how-to-do-it book to give a person the basic knowledge on how to help self and others through the rough spots in life. It consists of many individual sections—each one covering important situations in life, such as drug and alcohol problems, study difficulties, broken marriages, accidents and illnesses, a failing business, difficult children, and much more. This is the basic tool you need to help someone out of troubles, and bring about a happier life.

The Book of Case Remedies • *The Book of Case Remedies* gives you the exact and precise ways of getting bugged preclears and students really moving up the Bridge again. Ron developed, codified and released a formidable array of technical repair tools that auditors, Case Supervisors, Supervisors and even field staff members can apply on stalled preclears, students and even new public to get them winning. This book is a *must* for all Scientologists.

Research and Discovery Series • These volumes contain the only existing day-to-day, week-to-week record of the progress of L. Ron Hubbard's research in Dianetics and Scientology. Through the pages of these beautiful volumes you follow L. Ron Hubbard's fantastic research adventure, beginning in the depths of man's degradation and obsession with the material universe and soaring to the realms of the spirit, freed from the bondage of the past.

Technical Bulletins • These volumes contain all of L. Ron Hubbard's technical bulletins and issues from the earliest to the latest. Almost any technical question can be answered from the pages of these volumes, which also include an extremely extensive master subject index.

The Personal Achievement Series

The Personal Achievement Series cassettes are some of the all-time favorites among Ron's lectures. Beautifully packaged along with transcript and glossary, these lectures contain discoveries about the mind and life that you will want to always have on hand for your own use, and are also a perfect introduction to Dianetics and Scientology for friends and family.

The Story of Dianetics and Scientology • In this lecture, L. Ron Hubbard shares with you his earliest insights into human nature and gives a compelling and often humorous account of his experiences. Spend an unforgettable time with Ron as he talks about the start of Dianetics and Scientology!

The Road to Truth • The road to truth has eluded man since the beginning of time. In this classic lecture, L. Ron Hubbard explains what this road actually is and why it is the only road one MUST travel all the way once begun. This lecture reveals the only road to higher levels of living.

Scientology and Effective Knowledge • Voyage to new horizons of awareness! *Scientology and Effective Knowledge* by L. Ron Hubbard can help you understand more about yourself and others. A fascinating tale of the beginnings of Dianetics and Scientology.

The Deterioration of Liberty • What do governments fear so much in a population that they amass weapons to defend themselves from people? Find out from Ron in this classic lecture.

Power of Choice and Self-Determinism • Man's ability to determine the course of his life depends on his ability to exercise his power of choice. Find how you can increase your power of choice and self-determinism in life from Ron in this lecture.

Scientology and Ability • Ron points out that this universe is here because we perceive it and agree to it. Applying Scientology principles to life can bring new adventure to life and put you on the road to discovering better beingness.

The Hope of Man • Various men in history brought forth the idea that there was hope of improvement. But L. Ron Hubbard's discoveries in Dianetics and Scientology have made that hope a reality. Find out by listening to this lecture how Scientology has become man's one, true hope for his final freedom.

The Dynamics • In this lecture Ron gives incredible data on the dynamics: how man creates on them; what happens when a person gets stuck in just one; how wars relate to the third dynamic and much more.

Money • Ron talks in this classic lecture about that subject which makes or breaks men with the greatest of ease—money. Find out what money really is and gain greater control over your own finances.

Formulas for Success—*The Five Conditions* • How does one achieve real success? It sometimes appears that luck is the primary factor, but the truth of the matter is that natural laws exist which govern the conditions of life. These laws have been discovered by Ron, and in this lecture he gives you the exact steps to take in order to improve conditions in any aspect of your life.

Health and Certainty • You need certainty of yourself in order to achieve the success you want in life. In *Health and Certainty*, L. Ron Hubbard tells how you can achieve certainty and really be free to think for yourself. Get this tape now and start achieving your full potential!

Operation Manual for the Mind • Everybody has a mind—but who has an operation manual for it? This lecture reveals why man went on for thousands of years without understanding how his mind is supposed to work. The problem has been solved. Find out how with this tape.

Miracles • Why is it that man often loses to those forces he resists or opposes? Why can't an individual simply overcome obstacles in life and win? In the tape lecture *Miracles*, L. Ron Hubbard describes why one suffers losses in life. He also describes how a person can experience the miracles of happiness, self-fulfillment and winning at life. Get a copy today.

The Road to Perfection—*The Goodness of Man* • Unlike earlier practices that sought to "improve" man because he was "bad," Scientology assumes that you have *good* qualities that simply need to be *increased*. In *The Road to Perfection*, L. Ron Hubbard shows how workable this assumption really is—and how you can begin to use your mind, talents and abilities to the fullest. Get this lecture and increase your ability to handle life.

The Dynamic Principles of Existence • What does it take to survive in today's world? It's not something you learn much about in school. You have probably gotten a lot of advice about how to "get along." *Your survival right now is limited by the data you were given.* This lecture describes the dynamic principles of existence, and tells how you can use these principles to increase your success in all areas of life. Happiness and self-esteem *can* be yours. Don't settle for anything less.

Man: Good or Evil? • In this lecture, L. Ron Hubbard explores the greatest mystery that has confronted modern science and philosophy—the true nature of man's livingness and beingness. Is man simply a sort of wind-up doll or clock—or worse, an evil beast with no control of his cravings? Or is he capable of reaching higher levels of ability, awareness and happiness? Get this tape and find out the *real* answers.

Differences between Scientology and Other Studies • The most important questions in life are the ones you started asking as a child: What happens to a person when he dies? Is man basically good, or is he evil? What are the intentions of the world toward me? Did my mother and father really love me? What is love? Unlike other studies, which try to *force* you to think a certain way, Scientology enables you to find your own answers. Listen to this important lecture. It will put you on the road to true understanding and belief in yourself.

The Machinery of the Mind • We do a lot of things "automatically"—such as driving a car. But what happens when a person's mental machinery takes over and starts running him? In this fascinating lecture, L. Ron Hubbard gives you an understanding of what mental machinery really is, and how it can cause a person to lose control. You *can* regain your power of decision and be in full control of your life. Listen to this lecture and find out how.

The Affinity-Reality-Communication Triangle • Have you ever tried to talk to an angry man? Have you ever tried to get something across to someone who is really in fear? Have you ever known someone who was impossible to cheer up? Listen to this fascinating lecture by L. Ron Hubbard and learn how you can use the affinity-reality-communication triangle to resolve personal relationships. By using the data in this lecture, you can better understand others and live a happier life.

Increasing Efficiency • Inefficiency is a major barrier to success. How can you increase your efficiency? Is it a matter of changing your diet, or adjusting your working environment? These approaches have uniformly failed, because they overlook

the most important element: *you.* L. Ron Hubbard has found those factors that *can* increase your efficiency, and he reveals it in this timely lecture. Get *Increasing Efficiency* now, and start achieving *your* full potential.

Man's Relentless Search • For countless centuries, man has been trying to find himself. Why does this quest repeatedly end in frustration and disappointment? What is he *really* looking for, and why can't he find it? For the real truth about man and life, listen to this taped lecture by L. Ron Hubbard, *Man's Relentless Search.* Restore your belief in yourself!

More advanced books and lectures are available. Contact your nearest organization or write directly to the publisher for a full catalog.

Get Your Free Catalog
of Knowledge on
How to Improve Life

L. Ron Hubbard's books and tapes increase your ability to understand yourself and others. His works give you the practical know-how you need to improve your life and the lives of your family and friends.

Many more materials by L. Ron Hubbard are available than have been covered in the pages of this book. A free catalog of these materials is available on request.

Write for your free catalog today!

Bridge Publications, Inc.
4751 Fountain Avenue
Los Angeles, California 90029

NEW ERA® Publications International ApS
Store Kongensgade 55
1264 Copenhagen K, Denmark

"I am always happy to hear from my readers."

L. Ron Hubbard

These were the words of L. Ron Hubbard, who was always very interested in hearing from his friends and readers. He made a point of staying in communication with everyone he came in contact with over his fifty-year career as a professional writer, and he had thousands of fans and friends that he corresponded with all over the world.

The publishers of L. Ron Hubbard's works wish to continue this tradition and welcome letters and comments from you, his readers, both old and new.

Additionally, the publishers will be happy to send you information on anything you would like to know about Ron, his extraordinary life and accomplishments and the vast number of books he has written.

Any message addressed to the Author's Affairs Director at NEW ERA Publications International ApS will be given prompt and full attention.

NEW ERA Publications International ApS
Store Kongensgade 55
DK-1264 Copenhagen K
Denmark

Church and Organization Address List

United States of America

Albuquerque
Church of Scientology
8106 Menaul Blvd. N.E.
Albuquerque
New Mexico 87110

Ann Arbor
Church of Scientology
122 S. Main, Suite 160
Ann Arbor, Michigan 48106

Atlanta
Church of Scientology
2632 Piedmont Road, N.E.
Atlanta, Georgia 30324

Austin
Church of Scientology
2200 Guadalupe
Austin, Texas 78705

Boston
Church of Scientology
448 Beacon Street
Boston, Massachusetts 02115

Buffalo
Church of Scientology
47 West Huron Street
Buffalo, New York 14202

Chicago
Church of Scientology
3011 North Lincoln Avenue
Chicago, Illinois 60657

Cincinnati
Church of Scientology
215 West 4th Street, 5th Floor
Cincinnati, Ohio 45202

Clearwater
Church of Scientology
Flag® Service Organization
210 South Fort Harrison Avenue
Clearwater, Florida 34616

Columbus
Church of Scientology
167 East State Street
Columbus, Ohio 43215

Dallas
Church of Scientology
Celebrity Centre® Dallas
8501 Manderville Lane
Dallas, Texas 75231

Denver
Church of Scientology
375 South Navajo Street
Denver, Colorado 80223

Detroit
Church of Scientology
321 Williams Street
Royal Oak, Michigan 48067

Honolulu
Church of Scientology
1148 Bethel Street
Honolulu, Hawaii 96817

Kansas City
Church of Scientology
3619 Broadway
Kansas City, Missouri 64111

Las Vegas
Church of Scientology
846 East Sahara Avenue
Las Vegas, Nevada 89104

Church of Scientology
Celebrity Centre Las Vegas
1100 South 10th Street
Las Vegas, Nevada 89104

Long Island

Church of Scientology
99 Railroad Station Plaza
Hicksville, New York 11801

Los Angeles and vicinity

Church of Scientology
4810 Sunset Boulevard
Los Angeles, California 90027

Church of Scientology
1451 Irvine Boulevard
Tustin, California 92680

Church of Scientology
263 East Colorado Boulevard
Pasadena, California 91101

Church of Scientology
3619 West Magnolia Boulevard
Burbank, California 91506

Church of Scientology
American Saint Hill Organization
1413 North Berendo Street
Los Angeles, California 90027

Church of Scientology
American Saint Hill Foundation
1413 North Berendo Street
Los Angeles, California 90027

Church of Scientology
Advanced Organization of
  Los Angeles
1306 North Berendo Street
Los Angeles, California 90027

Church of Scientology
Celebrity Centre International
5930 Franklin Avenue
Hollywood, California 90028

Miami

Church of Scientology
120 Giralda Avenue
Coral Gables, Florida 33134

Minneapolis

Church of Scientology
1011 Nicollet Mall
Minneapolis, Minnesota 55403

Mountain View

Church of Scientology
2483 Old Middlefield Way
Mountain View
California 96043

New Haven

Church of Scientology
909 Whalley Avenue
New Haven, Connecticut 06515

New York City

Church of Scientology
227 West 46th Street
New York City, New York 10036

Church of Scientology
Celebrity Centre New York
65 East 82nd Street
New York City, New York 10036

Orlando

Church of Scientology
1830 East Colonial
Orlando, Florida 31802

Philadelphia

Church of Scientology
1315 Race Street
Philadelphia
Pennsylvania 19107

Phoenix

Church of Scientology
4450 North Central Avenue
  Suite 102
Phoenix, Arizona 85012

Portland

Church of Scientology
323 S.W. Washington
Portland, Oregon 97204

Church of Scientology
Celebrity Centre Portland
709 Southwest Salmon Street
Portland, Oregon 97205

Sacramento

Church of Scientology
825 15th Street
Sacramento, California 95814

Salt Lake City

Church of Scientology
1931 S. 100 East
Salt Lake City, Utah 84106

San Diego
Church of Scientology
635 "C" Street, Suite 200
San Diego, California 92101

San Francisco
Church of Scientology
83 McAllister Street
San Francisco, California 94102

San Jose
Church of Scientology
80 E. Rosemary
San Jose, California 95112

Santa Barbara
Church of Scientology
524 State Street
Santa Barbara
California 93101

Seattle
Church of Scientology
2603 3rd Avenue
Seattle, Washington 98121

St. Louis
Church of Scientology
9510 Page Boulevard
St. Louis, Missouri 63132

Tampa
Church of Scientology
3617 Henderson Blvd.
Tampa, Florida 33609

Washington, DC
Founding Church of
   Scientology of
   Washington, DC
2125 "S" Street N.W.
Washington, DC 20008

Church of Scientology
Celebrity Centre
   Washington, DC
4214 16th Street N.W.
Washington, DC 20011

Puerto Rico

Hato Rey
Church of Scientology
272 Avenue Central
Hyde Park, Hato Rey
Puerto Rico 00918

Canada

Edmonton
Church of Scientology
10187 112th St.
Edmonton, Alberta
Canada T5K 1M1

Kitchener
Church of Scientology
104 King St. West
Kitchener, Ontario
Canada N2G 2K6

Montreal
Church of Scientology
4489 Papineau Street
Montréal, Québec
Canada H2H 1T7

Ottawa
Church of Scientology
150 Rideau Street, 2nd Floor
Ottawa, Ontario
Canada K1N 5X6

Quebec
Church of Scientology
350 Bd Chareste Est
Québec, Québec
Canada G1K 3H5

Toronto
Church of Scientology
696 Yonge Street, 2nd Floor
Toronto, Ontario
Canada M4Y 2A7

Vancouver
Church of Scientology
401 West Hastings Street
Vancouver, British Columbia
Canada V6B 1L5

Winnipeg
Church of Scientology
Suite 125–388 Donald Street
Winnipeg, Manitoba
Canada R3B 2J4

United Kingdom

Birmingham
Church of Scientology
60–62 Constitution Hill
Birmingham
England B19 3JT

Brighton
Church of Scientology
5 St. Georges Place, London Road
Brighton, Sussex
England BN1 4GA

East Grinstead
Church of Scientology
  Saint Hill Foundation
Saint Hill Manor
East Grinstead, West Sussex
England RH19 4JY

Advanced Organization Saint Hill
Saint Hill Manor
East Grinstead, West Sussex
England RH19 4JY

Edinburgh
Hubbard Academy of
  Personal Independence
20 Southbridge
Edinburgh, Scotland
EH1 1LL

London
Church of Scientology
68 Tottenham Court Road
London, England W1P 0BB

Manchester
Church of Scientology
258 Deansgate
Manchester, England
M3 4BG

Plymouth
Church of Scientology
41 Ebrington Street
Plymouth, Devon
England PL4 9AA

Sunderland
Church of Scientology
51 Fawcett Street
Sunderland, Tyne and Wear
England SR1 1RS

Austria

Vienna
Church of Scientology
Schottenfeldgasse 13/15
1070 Wien, Austria

Church of Scientology
Celebrity Centre Vienna
Senefeldergasse 11/5
1100 Wien, Austria

Belgium

Brussels
Church of Scientology
61, rue du Prince Royal
1050 Bruxelles, Belgium

Denmark

Aarhus
Church of Scientology
Guldsmedegade 17, 2
8000 Århus C, Denmark

Copenhagen
Church of Scientology
Store Kongensgade 55
1264 København K, Denmark

Church of Scientology
Vesterbrogade 66B
1620 København V, Denmark

Church of Scientology
Advanced Organization
  Saint Hill for Europe and Africa
Jernbanegade 6
1608 København V, Denmark

France

Angers
Church of Scientology
10–12, rue Max Richard
49100 Angers, France

Clermont-Ferrand
Church of Scientology
1, rue Ballainvilliers
63000 Clermont-Ferrand, France

Lyon
Church of Scientology
3, place des Capucins
69001 Lyon, France

Paris
Church of Scientology
65, rue de Dunkerque
75009 Paris, France

Church of Scientology
Celebrity Centre Paris
69, rue Legendre
75017 Paris, France

St. Etienne
Church of Scientology
24, rue Marengo
42000 St. Etienne, France

Germany

Berlin
Church of Scientology
Sponholzstrasse 51/52
1000 Berlin 41, Germany

Düsseldorf
Church of Scientology
Friedrichstrasse 28
4000 Düsseldorf, Germany

Church of Scientology
Celebrity Centre Düsseldorf
Grupellostrasse 28
4000 Düsseldorf, Germany

Frankfurt
Church of Scientology
Darmstädter Landstrasse 213
6000 Frankfurt 70, Germany

Hamburg
Church of Scientology
Steindamm 63
2000 Hamburg 1, Germany

Church of Scientology
Celebrity Centre Hamburg
Steindamm 70
2000 Hamburg 1, Germany

Hanover
Church of Scientology
Hubertusstrasse 2
3000 Hannover 1, Germany

Munich
Church of Scientology
Beichstrasse 12
8000 München 40, Germany

Stuttgart
Church of Scientology
Urbanstrasse 70
7000 Stuttgart 1, Germany

Israel

Tel Aviv
Dianetics and Scientology College
42 Gorden Street, 2nd Floor
Tel Aviv 66023, Israel

Italy

Brescia
Church of Scientology
Via Fratelli Bronzetti, 20
25125 Brescia, Italy

Catania
Church of Scientology
Via Giuseppe Garibaldi, 9
95121 Catania, Italy

Milan
Church of Scientology
Via Abetone, 10
20137 Milano, Italy

Monza
Church of Scientology
Via Cavour, 5
20052 Monza, Italy

Novara
Church of Scientology
Corso Cavallotti, 7
28100 Novara, Italy

Nuoro
Church of Scientology
Via Lamarmora, 115
08100 Nuoro, Italy

Padua
Church of Scientology
Via Mameli, 5
35131 Padova, Italy

Pordenone
Church of Scientology
Via Montereale, 10/C
33170 Pordenone, Italy

Rome
Church of Scientology
Via Della Pineta Sacchetti, 201
00185 Roma, Italy

Turin
Church of Scientology
Via Guarini, 4
10121 Torino, Italy

Verona
Church of Scientology
Via Teatro Filarmonico, 3
37121 Verona, Italy

Netherlands

Amsterdam
Church of Scientology
Nieuwe Zijds Voorburgwal 271
1012 RL Amsterdam, Netherlands

Norway

Oslo
Church of Scientology
Storgata 9
0155 Oslo 1, Norway

Portugal

Lisbon
Instituto de Dianética
Rua Actor Taborda 39–5°
1000 Lisboa, Portugal

Spain

Barcelona
Asociación Civil de Dianética
Calle Pau Clarís 85,
   Principal dcha.
08010 Barcelona, Spain

Madrid
Asociación Civil de Dianética
Montera 20, Piso 1° dcha.
28013 Madrid, Spain

Sweden

Göteborg
Church of Scientology
Odinsgatan 8, 2 tr.
411 03 Göteborg, Sweden

Malmö
Church of Scientology
Lantmannagatan 62 C
214 48 Malmö, Sweden

Stockholm
Church of Scientology
St. Eriksgatan 56
112 34 Stockholm, Sweden

Switzerland

Basel
Church of Scientology
Herrengrabenweg 56
4054 Basel, Switzerland

Bern
Church of Scientology
Dammweg 29
Postfach 352
3000 Bern 11, Switzerland

Geneva
Church of Scientology
Route de Saint-Julien 7–9
C.P. 823
1227 Carouge
Switzerland

Lausanne
Church of Scientology
10, rue de la Madeleine
1003 Lausanne, Switzerland

Zurich
Church of Scientology
Badenerstrasse 141
8004 Zürich, Switzerland

Australia

Adelaide
Church of Scientology
24–28 Waymouth Street
Adelaide, South Australia 5000
Australia

Brisbane
Church of Scientology
106 Edward Street
Brisbane, Queensland 4000
Australia

Canberra
Church of Scientology
108 Bunda Street, Suite 16
Civic Canberra
A.C.T. 2601, Australia

Melbourne
Church of Scientology
42–44 Russell Street
Melbourne, Victoria 3000
Australia

Perth
Church of Scientology
39–41 King Street
Perth, Western Australia 6000
Australia

Sydney
Church of Scientology
201 Castlereagh Street
Sydney, New South Wales 2000
Australia

Church of Scientology
Advanced Organization
  Saint Hill Australia,
  New Zealand and Oceania
19–37 Greek Street
Glebe, New South Wales 2037
Australia

Japan

Tokyo
Scientology Organization
1-23-1 Higashi-Gotanda
Shinagawa-ku
Tokyo, Japan 141

New Zealand

Auckland
Church of Scientology
32 Lorne Street
Auckland 1, New Zealand

Africa

Bulawayo
Church of Scientology
Southampton House, Suite 202
Main Street and 9th Ave.
Bulawayo, Zimbabwe

Cape Town
Church of Scientology
St. Georges Centre, 2nd Floor
13 Hout Street
Cape Town 8001, South Africa

Durban
Church of Scientology
57 College Lane
Durban 4001, South Africa

Harare
Church of Scientology
State Lottery Building
  First Floor
PO Box 3524
Corner Speke Avenue
  and Julius Nyerere Way
Harare, Zimbabwe

Johannesburg
Church of Scientology
Security Building, 2nd Floor
95 Commissioner Street
Johannesburg 2001
South Africa

Church of Scientology
101 Huntford Building
Corner Hunter and Fortesque Roads
Yeoville, Johannesburg 2198
South Africa

Port Elizabeth
Church of Scientology
2 St. Christopher Place
27 Westbourne Road Central
Port Elizabeth 6001
South Africa

Pretoria
Church of Scientology
City Centre, 1st Floor
272 Pretorius Street
Pretoria 0002
South Africa

Colombia

Bogotá
Centro Cultural de Dianética
Calle 95 No. 19-A-28
Barrio Chicó
Bogotá, Colombia

Mexico

Guadalajara
Organización Cultural Dianética
  de Guadalajara, A.C.
Pedro Moreno #1078 Int 3
Sector Juárez
Guadalajara, Jalisco, México

Mexico City
Asociación Cultural Dianética, A.C.
Avenida Revolución #1359
Colonia Campestre
C.P. 01040 México, D.F.

Instituto de Filosofía Aplicada, A.C.
Durango #105
Colonia Roma
C.P. 06700 México, D.F.

Instituto de Filosofía Aplicada, A.C.
Anaxágoras #231
Colonia Narvarte
C.P. 03020 México, D.F.

Instituto Tecnológico
de Dianética, A.C.
Avenida Nuevo León 238
Colonia Hipódromo Condesa
C.P. 06170 México, D.F.

Organización Desarrollo
y Dianética, A.C.
Sánchez Azcona #403, 4° Piso
Colonia Narvarte
C.P. 03020 México, D.F.

Organización Cultural
Dianética, A.C.
Nicolás San Juan #1734
Colonia Del Valle
C.P. 03100 México, D.F.

Venezuela

Caracas
Asociación Cultural
Dianética de Venezuela, A.C.
Avenida Principal de las Palmas,
Cruce Con Avenida Carupano
Quinta Suha, Las Palmas
Caracas, Venezuela

Valencia
Asociación Cultural
Dianética de Venezuela, A.C.
Avenida 101 No. 150-23
Urbanización La Alegría
Apartado Postal 833
Valencia, Venezuela

To obtain any books or cassettes by L. Ron Hubbard which are not available at your local organization, contact any of the following publishers:

Bridge Publications, Inc.
4751 Fountain Avenue
Los Angeles, California 90029

Continental Publications
Liaison Office
696 Yonge Street
Toronto, Ontario
Canada M4Y 2A7

NEW ERA Publications
International ApS
Store Kongensgade 55
1264 København K, Denmark

ERA DINÁMICA EDITORES,
S.A. de C.V.
Nicolás San Juan No. 208
Colonia Narvarte
C.P. 03020 México, D.F.

NEW ERA Publications, Ltd.
78 Holmethorpe Avenue
Redhill, Surrey
England RH1 2NL

NEW ERA Publications
Australia Pty Ltd.
68–72 Wentworth Ave.
Sydney 2000
Australia

Continental Publications Pty Ltd.
PO Box 27080
Benrose
2011 South Africa

NEW ERA Publications
Italia Srl
Via L.G. Columella, 12
20128 Milano, Italy

NEW ERA Publications
Deutschland GmbH
Bahnhofstrasse 40
2153 Neu Wulmstorf
Germany

NEW ERA Publications France
111, boulevard de Magenta
75010 Paris, France

NEW ERA Publications
España, S.A.
C/De la Paz, 4, entpta dcha.
28012 Madrid, Spain

NEW ERA Publications
Japan, Inc.
5-4-5-803 Nishi-Gotanda
Shinagawa-ku
Tokyo, Japan 141